TORTURED CARDBOARD

HOW GREAT BOARD GAMES ARISE FROM CHAOS, SURVIVE BY CHANCE, IMPART WISDOM, AND GAIN IMMORTALITY

PHILIP E. ORBANES
(WITH THE GAMES GNOME)

PERMUTED
PRESS

A PERMUTED PRESS BOOK
ISBN: 978-1-68261-853-0
ISBN (eBook): 978-1-68261-854-7

Cover Design by Cody Corcoran

PERMUTED
PRESS

Permuted Press, LLC
New York • Nashville
permutedpress.com

Published in the United States of America

This book is dedicated to Anna and Sybille…
and also Leo and Kyle who epitomize
game fans everywhere.

CONTENTS

INTRODUCTION

ike many of its colorful terms, "tortured cardboard" was coined by those who disparage the board game industry and regard it as trivial. Nevertheless, those of us inside the business find this idiom endearing. We know board games reflect whatever "tortures" culture. Study board games and you know what's ticking in society. It's been so for five thousand years. My friend, the "Games Gnome," tells me this.

While paintings, literature, and musical compositions can achieve the status of fine art, great board games are equally deserving of this accolade, because in addition to artistic appeal, they must provide a new experience each time played. They are *interactive* art—art that changes with use, according to who is doing the "changing" (playing the game).

The term "tortured" cardboard sums up what happens to cardboard when making a board game. It gets cut, "scored" (incised), bent, perforated, punched, gouged, bound, folded, glued, papered over—and ends up looking nothing like its beginnings. Perfectly Medieval! And also, a perfect metaphor for every gyration, distortion, and conflict that comes and goes in real life. Such aberrations typically engender a flood of new board games—one or more of which will survive this latest upheaval and carry on forever. Why? And more importantly, why should *you* be interested? As the Games Gnome asserts, it's because great games are replete with lessons applicable to achievement in *your* life. Straightforward lessons, not tortuous, and free of the usual pain when learned "the hard way."

As the twenty-first century gathers momentum, our love affair with board games continues to strengthen. Despite the rise of digital games, board game sales have steadily increased, because they fill a gaping void created by reduced social contact (hello, iPhones). My wise friend, the Games Gnome, commenting on the merits of playing a board game while surrounded by family and friends whimsically says, "Like sunshine, beneficial it is." Take it from me; he is the Yoda of the games world. He will be here shortly.

I better let you in on something. The Gnome is "different" and he's not just popping-in. He's planned an adventure and it has to do with those lessons he's so worked up about. "It is better to experience these, firsthand," he tells me. "They hit harder; you won't forget them." I suspect there will be no stay-at-home lecture, no textbook recitation, no blah-blah-blah. We're going places. Heaven knows where, but that's okay. I'm up for a journey. After all, I am naturally curious *and* I also see life as a grand game.

Truth is, I've always loved games. I began inventing them when I was a kid and eventually became a game industry executive and historian. Naturally, I get accused of "playing games" for a living (*I plead guilty*). I've been accused of having too much fun (*guilty, again*). And I've been accused of accomplishing nothing of real value (*hold on, not guilty!*).

Here's the thing. It's not me that matters; it's the *products* I've produced, touched, or influenced. And, as it turns out, some of them have tremendous worth to a whole lot of people (even if they don't realize it). As the Games Gnome likes to opine, "Play the game, or the game plays you." *Really?* I am reminded of what Carl Jung, the Swiss psychiatrist and philosopher, once wrote (I'll use italics because this is really important):

The world will ask you who you are, and if you don't know, the world will tell you.

Hello Carl!

"Yes, truth." The Games Gnome has arrived. (He is taller than you might expect, not your garden variety gnome.) He sets down his worn cloth bag, takes off his colorful hat, and seats himself across the game board. He contemplates his first move and says, "There is important philosophy in the realm of board games. It reflects the daily uncertainty we experience in the world at large and offers advice on how to contend with it."

Play the Game, or the Game Plays You!

Philosophy? I try not to go over the top with such lofty talk. I mean, Pythagoras likely coined the term 2,600 years ago when board games were still made of stone and wood. But I concede this point to the Gnome, because philosophy tackles problems related to knowledge, reason, language, thought, and the Big One (existence itself). The best board games immerse you, the player, in a metaphor of all these (except perhaps existence). I convey this conclusion to the Games Gnome. He strokes his beard and glows.

"You're on the right path." Then he adds a qualification, "Of course, I'm not talking about *all* board games, many of which are disposable like trash or vacuous like situation comedies. Or ill-conceived like most political ideas. I won't go there. I'm talking about those that will live well beyond my expected long lifetime and yours."

The Gnome believes he knows pretty much everything about games. For starters, he's been studying games for a long time. He plays, he collects, he invents, he writes, and edits. Unlike me, he is not tied down. He travels at will and prefers to show up in mid-morning expecting to see a tray of my wife's irresistible peanut butter cookies popping out of the oven, like today. She accepts his warm greetings and joins us at the table. We talk games over cookies and coffee. "Yes, a select few games have become timeless," says the Gnome.

"Like chess, backgammon, Scrabble®, and Monopoly®," I offer.

"And a dozen more whose immortality was achieved through merit, not whim or impulse."

I have my opinions, of course. I've lived the life of a games-man since college. I've worked with countless men and women who made the industry hum for decades. I've met the luminaries: the creators, makers, promoters—and the occasional egotist who thwarts progress (for a while, at least). I've learned something about board games from each of them. Along the way, I've pondered whimsical questions like: What exactly is cardboard? Why is it tortured and who is doing the torturing? And more seriously, what precisely is a game? (This word is thrown around indiscriminately, like a ball in a stadium.)

A hundred years ago, Carl Jung wrote, "One of the most difficult tasks men can perform…is the invention of good games, and it cannot be done by men out of touch with their instinctive selves." If Jung were with us today, he'd likely be inclusive and would write "men and women." Many women play a key role in the creation and success of modern board games. But aside from that, I'm with Jung. To be a successful games inventor, you need to have instinct. The game industry's first rule is: *Rules are meant to be broken.* They are best broken by creative people unaware, or in defiance of, preexisting rules that set forth what makes a good game. But enough of that.

Today, I have a visitor who's come to offer his own philosophy. I politely express interest, "Mr. Gnome, why do you believe some games are gifts to humankind? What lies beneath the surface of their boards, the wording of their rules, that makes them so special?"

The Games Gnome rubs two fingers together, moves his game piece, and replies, "Every one of these remarkable creations came about because of chaos and chance. They were conceived in stressful times and gained a foothold because random events prevented an early death." I comprehend the latter; most games survive for one year or less in the marketplace. He continues, "After each of these games took root, it became apparent it offered something beneficial beyond the game board and that is why it stuck around."

"And imparted the lessons you speak of, right?"

His grin affirms. He adds, as an aside, "All of my wisdom I got through playing games."

"Metaphysical wisdom?" I ask. I am thinking of Jung and his kind.

The Gnome frowns. "Look, Phil, no game is going to live forever if all it imparts is abstract, highly theoretical head scratching! I mean practical wisdom. I've come here to reveal how these morsels comprise a whole. Each immortal game contributes something to a compact body of keen insight."

"Let's take it a step at a time. Give me one game as an example."

"How about the game we're sharing right now?"

We're playing Clue®, the great detective game. I think for a moment. "Fair enough, Games Gnome. Clue is timeless. Let's talk about its lessons, like…"

My wife, Anna, interrupts. She's curious by the Gnome's first claim and interjects, "But where do chaos and chance come in?"

The Gnome sets down his hand of cards, eager to exploit the opening Anna has provided. His eyes twinkle as he chants, "Chaos, chance, Clue. Chaos, chance, Clue…. Your husband should be able to answer your question after he and I take a little trip." He returns to the game and makes his first suggestion: *Professor Plum in the Conservatory with the Knife.*

"You'll need to help him pack. We're leaving this evening."

Anna looks startled. "You mean, just like that? On a whim? Aren't air tickets expensive if not purchased well in advance?"

The Gnome reassures her, "Not to worry, I have more frequent flyer miles than I know what to do with. Besides, there's no better way to grasp chaos than to experience it firsthand." He reaches into his bag and produces two business class tickets. "It is most helpful in life to think two moves ahead, just like in a game." The Gnome likes to boast that he possesses "gamer's anticipation."

I show him the Knife card from my hand. Suggestion refuted. I look at Anna and shrug. "It's something I have to do," I tell her. She is understanding; I am blessed. I turn to the Gnome, "Where are we going?"

His blue eyes brighten once more. "England. You'll need your passport."

England? Although I've known the Gnome for many years, he remains, in large part, a mystery to me. I have only a vague idea of where he lives, and wonder seriously about his ancestry. I've never traveled with him, so I sense opportunity. A trip might reveal what has been hidden from my view, much like the secrets uncovered during the Clue game we are playing.

The following morning, I find myself trailing behind the Gnome, as we dash through London's Heathrow Airport.

The gleaming terminal is packed with travelers scurrying for their gates. An international stew of languages is heard—a global radio dial. The abbreviated night across five different time zones has fogged my head. But the Gnome is not afflicted. He points to the British Air departure board. "Gate D-Fourteen. Come on Phil, we're going to visit the Brums."

Did I mishear? Brums? "Did you mean Bums?" I ask.

"No, you heard me right. The Brums."

Birmingham is England's second largest city; it is as far from London as Philadelphia is from Washington, DC. The city's original name was Brummagem, or Bromwichham. Whichever, it led to the town folks calling themselves "Brummies" or "Brums" for short. So says the Gnome.

The sun greets us after we collect our bags. My friend provides directions to a taxi driver, who speeds out of the airport bearing left at the turnabout, causing my heart to stop momentarily. (I've been to England dozens of times but remain disoriented by the practice of driving on the "wrong side" of the road.) In England, a predictable sameness paints the scenery between airport and center city: cottages, small farms, pastures, old shops, and then gritty buildup. Birmingham adheres to this recipe.

We've come to this green and pleasant land on a day in May in search of the late Anthony Pratt—the Brum who invented Clue (or "Cluedo®" as it is known in his native country).

CHAPTER ONE

UNRAVELING A CLUE

Birmingham is not meant to delight the eye, it being industrial. The Gnome tells me it is in fact the *birthplace* of industry and is still very much working class. Over there, a Jaguar auto plant ("jag-you-are," as the Brits pronounce it). Over here, MG. The main road snakes through downtown; our taxi negotiates a shopping area known as the "Bullring" where the big Selfridges department store is covered with fifteen thousand aluminum ("owl-you-min-ee-um") discs. Enough said.

We pause at a quaint bed and breakfast (the Gnome has made reservations), freshen up, and set out for a neighborhood known as Balsall Heath (heath=scrublands) that, remarkably, was hit by a tornado in 2005. *(Tornado? In England?)* It's rebuilt now: rows of two-story terraced homes made of red brick, topped by slate roofs, all connected, all mirror images of the ones across the street. Today, this neighborhood is heavily Muslim.

I think about the Gnome's "chaos." I see no outward sign of disorder here. I say so.

"But there was in Anthony Pratt's time," the Gnome explains. "Back then, life was completely dysfunctional. The Luftwaffe was bombing the life out of Birmingham by night, trying to destroy its industrial might. You see, the factories had switched to making tanks and military vehicles, so Birmingham became a prime target during the Blitz. Hysteria, misery, and disorder were the norm. Incendiaries ignited countless fires, which the Brums fought until morning, then cleared rumble and found a way to get the factories working again. Of course, everything they cherished before the war—the theaters, shops, and markets—were also obliterated. More importantly, so was the water supply and electricity. That, my friend, was chaos, pure and simple."

I look back in the direction of the car factories and try to imagine orange flames licking the sky over a blacked-out city. One can tell himself there were explosions and giant flames, but one cannot *feel* the awe and fear they instill. I voice this realization, but the Gnome does not hear me. Something is happening to him. He becomes rigid, as if entering a trance.

"I see it," he says in a hushed voice, "just the way it was. April ninth, 1941. Fires are everywhere in the center of town. Hundreds of them. The noise is deafening. Explosions, sirens, screams."

"You mean you are visualizing what it was like," I suggest.

"No," the Gnome replies firmly. "I actually *see* it happening. I have this ability."

"You can experience the past, actually witness it?" Is this possible? I wonder. Well, I always felt the Gnome was "different." Here is proof.

He nods silently.

"Can you see the future too?" I ask hesitantly.

The Gnome shakes his head. "No, I only have a rearview mirror. It's a trait passed down through the genes of my line, on my mother's side. All gnomes inherit something rather extraordinary. My father gave me my height."

I am curious about the Gnome's genealogy, but this is neither the time nor place.

"Follow me." He begins to walk briskly, oblivious to the passersby. He leads me into an alley and halts before a window; paint is peeling off its sill. The Gnome speaks in a monotone. "We are standing on what was once his driveway. I see him in the kitchen inside. And his wife." He is referring to Anthony and Elva Pratt. "They are huddled over the kitchen table. Under the candlelight, I see her pencil sketching the layout of a mansion on a big piece of paper. He's got a cigarette dangling from his lips as he cuts cards out of a piece of cardboard with a big pair of shears. I believe they are making the first version of the game. The process is just beginning."

"Wouldn't they be in a shelter? You tell me scores of bombs are falling just a couple of miles away."

"Your friend, Carl Jung, said, 'In all chaos there is a cosmos.' Pratt is sick and tired of the war. He's resigned to his fate. He picks the way through rubble every day to report to work. He has now found his cosmos; it is a game he is inventing in defiance of it all."

I can't see through this window; its shade is drawn. "What're they like...back then?" I ask hesitantly.

"She's pretty; a brunette. He's bespectacled, very thick round lenses. Thinning hair. A bit on the husky side. Pleasant looking fellow. Graceful fingers. Did you know he was a pianist before the war? Played in country hotels. Traveled around a lot. Even on cruise ships. Very much in demand. The war changed all that. Bad eyesight kept him out of the military, so instead, he works a drill press making tank parts. Pure tedium, and always rush-rush."

I picture a misfit drill press operator in a noisy factory.

The Gnome looks to his left. "I see his motor car back there, gathering dust. There is no gasoline for pleasure travel. Alas, the Pratts are stuck at home, and this note of disorder leads to boredom. But it also leads to escape, because it compelled them to craft what becomes the Clue game. And Pratt knew what it should be like, from the get-go."

"Tell me more."

"Before the war, when Tony was tinkling the ivories in rural hotels, a party game entitled 'Murder' would frequently be played for entertainment. The guests were challenged to figure out the mystery, namely, who among them had secretly been assigned the role of the murderer. Pratt enjoyed these games immensely. And, of course, he and Elva loved to read murder mystery novels."

My wife is a big fan of Agatha Christie, so I know Dame Agatha's first mystery was published in 1920, twenty-one years earlier.

"One day, the Pratts decide: war be damned—why not make a game that would play like 'Murder' and draw upon the plots and settings typically found in an Agatha Christie mystery? Easier said than done, of course, because the great challenge was to make sure the crime's solution would be different every time their game was played, unlike a Christie novel with its permanent ending."

"That's one of the reasons board games remain popular. A different outcome every time.

Clue is exemplary."

The Gnome looks through the window once more. "They are not yet calling their game Clue or Cluedo. Elva has just picked up a notebook and is writing in it while her husband dictates. I can see a label on the cover. Written in India ink is the name 'Murder at Tudor Close.'"

"So where did the name Clue—or Cluedo—come from?"

The Gnome takes a deep breath, shudders, and returns to the present.

"Let's find out. Time to travel a little further."

A taxi drops us off at another alley, this one close to the center of town. The surrounding buildings cast it in deep shadow. I see nothing as we enter the darkness; I feel a certain foreboding. But the Gnome is nonplussed. Suddenly, there appears a wooden door on our right, illuminated by a pale yellow light. An inscribed brass plaque appears on the door: The Cluedo Club. I notice a window on its left. I peer in. There is life inside.

Like many of the clubs I've been invited to in London, this one reminds me of a library from the nineteenth century. Dark paneling, lots of portraits hanging on the walls, recessed shelves filled with books and bric-a-brac, and the ubiquitous English bar at the far end. In the center of it all are four handsome tables with carved legs, each surrounded by four baize-cushioned chairs. The tabletops each feature a recessed Cluedo game board under glass.

"This club is packed come nightfall," the Gnome offers. Right now, as noon approaches, only one game is ongoing. But its foursome pays us no mind, concentrating instead on their game, their ales, and layered sandwiches.

"Ah, there comes Eric," the Gnome says with a wave. "He's the proprietor. And a genuine Cluedo Master."

"Good to see you, old chap," says Eric, who reminds me of a throwback English teacher: Spectacles, bushy white sideburns, pleasant little mouth, and a prosperous belly dressed in tweed.

"Who's the bloke?" Eric asks. The Gnome introduces me.

Eric serves a lovely lunch. I ask questions as we munch. Yes, the club has been here for some time. Yes, it does tend to remind the Brums that Cluedo was born in their factory city. Yes, there is more to the game than meets the eye. Cluedo is deep.

The English game board is rather stark, its nine rooms lacking the lovely top-down furnishings and floorings of the American version.

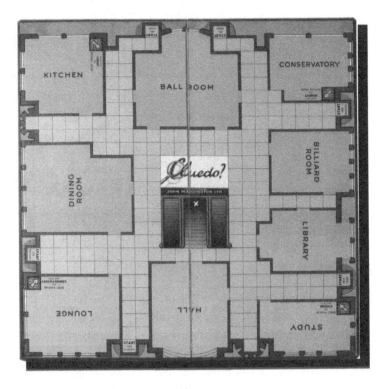

The weapons and suspects are quite familiar, except for the inclusion of a "Reverend Green" as opposed to "Mr. Green."

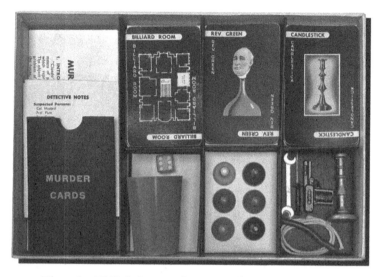

Photo by Phil Orbanes of game in the Strong Museum

Eric points to a framed box cover on the wall. "The original package," he notes,

> *"was a rather humble black and white affair, with the sole embellishment of a red fingerprint. And this bloody print was removed in subsequent print runs. Bloody smart move, by the way, because the merchants on the High Street were squeamish about promoting murder as entertainment."*

Photo by Phil Orbanes of game in the Strong Museum

Like most game boxes of its era, the package is small—only big enough to house the game's components. The board came separately and featured a label on its rear side whose graphic matched that on the package, presumably so a store clerk would match the correct game board with the utensils box when making a sale.

Most notably, the name of the game is not "Murder at Tudor Close" or even "Clue."

It is a made-up word: "Cluedo." I am about to ask about this curiosity when the Gnome pipes up. "I've shown you the chaos. Now, let's talk about the role chance played in keeping Cluedo going long enough for it to catch on." He turns towards Eric and gestures. "You're on."

Eric Sommersby responds, "To demonstrate the significance of chance in the survival of Cluedo, I'm going to toss the game's die six times. What do you think the odds are that I will roll all six of its numbers?"

I don't know the answer offhand, but I know the method to arrive at it (Probability and Statistics class to the rescue). I ask Eric if he has a calculator; one is produced from behind the bar. "Multiply one times point eighty-three, times point sixty-seven, times point fifty, times point thirty-three, times point seventy." His fingers tap the keys. Eric announces, "Fifteen point six."

"So the odds of rolling six different numbers, in six throws, with one die, is slim—under sixteen percent."

"Precisely my point," says Eric. "Pratt literally had to roll six different numbers in six goes to put Cluedo over. Would you like to know what each throw signifies?"

"Of course."

Eric tells us the following.

Having perfected Murder at Tudor Close by 1944, Pratt became obsessed with worry that someone who happened to see his game would "lift" it. Following advice from a friend, Pratt applied for and received a design patent for his game.

Pratt's game had no practical value until it found a publisher. A month later, he chanced upon a former mate who happened to have invented a popular game named Buccaneer, which was published by England's leading game company, the John Waddington Company.

In February of 1945, Anthony and Elva Pratt took a northbound train to Leeds, 114 miles distant, and met with Norman Watson, the managing director of the firm. Waddingtons, it turned out, was primarily a printer and maker of packaging. The firm had gotten into game-making almost by chance. And while it had become England's top game and playing card producer, the war was still going on; satisfying the government's printing orders and edicts precluded new game production.

But Norman Watson instinctively liked what he saw and played. He agreed to consider publishing the game after the war but insisted on a different name. While "murder" may be an acceptable word in a theatrical or mystery book title, Watson did not believe the game trade would stock a game with "murder" in its name. Pratt demurred and permitted Watson and his staff to think of a new one. For a while, nothing worthy arose and consideration of the game almost ended. Then Watson coined a name that everyone liked: "Cluedo"— being a combination of two words: "clue" and "ludo." "Ludo" being the name for Parcheesi in England; in Latin, it means "I play." (Victor, Norman's quick-witted son, once told me, "Dad loved to play with words almost as much as he loved to play with life.")

Yet with the end of the war, Cluedo could not "get off the ground" as Watson lamented. Of all things, cardboard—the most essential material in the production of a board game—remained on ration in England. This shortage of cardboard would endure for four years. (While the United States quickly, if fitfully, returned to a booming peacetime economy, war-scarred England did not.)

Norman Watson, frustrated, decided to offer Cluedo to his American partners, the great Parker Brothers game company in Salem, Massachusetts. By 1948, the firm's founder, George Parker, was suffering from what nowadays is known as Alzheimer's disease. Control of the firm was in the hands of his son-in-law and nephews. They did not accept Parker's long-standing rule that his firm would, like Waddingtons, publish no game about murdering people. Son-in-law Robert Barton believed that Scotland Yard, Agatha Christie, and London's East End theaters were synonymous with great mysteries, including murders, and the game could succeed in America if its English appearance were maintained. And of course, if the name were "Clue" rather than "Cluedo." To further soften Clue's murderous theme, its rules referred to "The Act" instead of a murder, which all players would attempt to solve.

Only after these six hurdles were surmounted, did Anthony Pratt's game finally appear on the market, albeit one 3,500 miles from his home. A few months later, in the fall of 1949, the initial success of "Clue—The Great Detective Game" inspired confidence for Waddington to divert some of its cardboard stock to the manufacture of Cluedo.

During the time Eric told this tale of chance, we'd been playing the game. Doing so reminded me of the first time I played at age nine, having persuaded my mother to buy a copy for me. She was a mystery fan and loved the game for its evocation of Agatha Christie. Me? I didn't yet know a mystery from a mole hole.

What I liked was the *idea* behind the game. The process of deduction needed to make sense of clues gathered during play and figure out what three cards were hiding in the "Solution" envelope placed on the central staircase of the game board. My token that day, as today, was Colonel Mustard. Eric favors Professor Plum, while the Gnome is Miss Scarlet ("Red is my favorite color").

Beyond the tokens, there are five little metallic weapons—such as a lead pipe, revolver, and candlestick—and a piece of real rope (it became plastic in later editions), plus a deck of twenty-one cards, one for each suspect, weapon, and room on the game board. Three of these cards form the solution; the remaining eighteen cards are dealt out. Those you receive (kept hidden from your opponents) are surely not part of the solution. The trick then is to figure out the cards held by your opponents to arrive at the correct solution prior to any of your opponents doing so.

And so, we roll the dice, move our tokens through the hallways of the mansion and offer a "suggestion" upon entering a room—making a guess as to what three cards comprise the solution. The player on the left has first dibs of disproving your suggestion by privately revealing one of the cards you named.

As the game progresses, I find myself checking off more and more suspects, weapons, and rooms on my Detective Notes sheet. To confuse my opponents, I sometimes suggest the name of a card I am holding in hand. The Gnome seems perplexed; Eric remains stone-faced. I can't read him. I don't know if he is miles away from solving the crime, or ready to pounce.

An imposing grandfather clock ticks away in the corner. When its hands have advanced by forty-one minutes, stone-faced Eric becomes Mister Excitement. "I've got it! I will solve the crime. Reverend Green in the Kitchen with the Candlestick."

I, too, am certain about the Kitchen and the Candlestick, but I am still debating Mrs. Peacock versus Reverend Green. *How can Eric be positive it was Green?* Grinning merrily, Eric picks up the envelope and tilts it on end. Out drops the Kitchen, the Candlestick, and the nasty Reverend. Eric exclaims offhandedly, "Good game, gents. Really good game." He is already reaching into his pocket, producing a little notebook. He flips to a specific page and makes an entry. "I've been keeping a diary of every game I play. My goal is to eventually play all three hundred twenty-four different mysteries." I understand: nine rooms, nine weapons and six suspects provide for 324 combinations. "As of today, I have only twenty-three to go." Eric has obviously played *a lot* of games of Cluedo.

The Gnome speaks. "I think Phil tried to confuse me by naming the Ballroom twice, which he obviously was holding in hand. But tell me, Eric, how did you figure out it was Green and not Peacock?"

"Simple, my friend. I listened to who you two were suggesting, and not suggesting, and deduced it couldn't be Peacock."

"Brilliant!" This seems to be a moment the Gnome has anticipated. "Your deduction reveals Clue's first great lesson applicable to life: Benefit from what you get for free."

"Do explain," says Eric, his victor's smile still radiating.

"If you put aside your emotions and watch people without prejudice as they interact, you will detect where their zone of confidence lies, and also where they feel vulnerable. Now, let's say you're looking to accomplish something that requires the cooperation of another. You ought to know which buttons to press, right? And which ones to avoid."

"What else do you think my favorite game teaches?" Eric asks.

"Don't follow a straight line when there's a faster way to your goal. I call it the 'Long is Short' rule."

"Come again?" I say.

"Phil, think back to those times in the game when you were heading for a specific room, and suddenly, one of us whisked your token to a room, far removed, to make a suggestion. How did you react?"

The Gnome is referring to one of Clue's more dramatic rules: The token and weapon named in a suggestion must be moved into the room where an opponent makes a suggestion. "Well, you messed up my plans. But I couldn't afford to waste the time trying to go back, so I entered the nearest room on my next turn to make a suggestion, even though I had already eliminated this room from contention. At least I learned something valuable about the weapon or suspect."

The Gnome is pleased. "Spoken like a true game player. Now, in life, it is natural to try and proceed logically, step by step. You plan your day, not expecting to be disrupted. You envision a series of logical promotions to reach your dream job. But distractions and setbacks appear all too frequently. Best laid plans, and all. However, not only do you encounter setbacks, a few choice opportunities come within grasp. They also beckon you to deviate. So the long way is actually the shorter way if you can move faster."

Eric interjects, "If you step outside yourself and calmly evaluate the possibilities each diversion poses, you might gain from the detour. This is exactly what Clue teaches."

I think of a friend. "We all knew Victor Watson, right?" (Victor agilely ran Waddingtons for many years after his father, Norman, retired.) "I once asked him what the key to his success was. Victor replied, 'I learned to jump through the window when it opened, which was seldom when I was ready to jump.'"

"Your mention, Eric, of stepping outside oneself. That reminds me of something Carl Jung said. He said that 'your vision will become clear only when you can step aside and look into your own heart.'"

The Gnome laughs. "Sorry, Eric, but Phil has had Jung on his mind ever since I raised the topic of philosophy with him."

Eric nods and says, "Jung was also a games fan." He then voices the conclusion of this Jung quote, "He who looks outside, dreams; who looks inside, awakes."

The Gnome offers his take, "There's no benefit in being stubborn. If you can learn to objectively evaluate decisions, you greatly improve your chance of winning any board game or taking a step forward in the Big Game."

"Let's wrap it up now," says the Games Gnome. "Clue's final lesson is actually universal to most games. But Phil, since this is the first one we've analyzed, I'll voice it here: Figure out your goal and always aim for it."

"Oh, how true," says Eric resolutely. "As you know, there are three hundred twenty-four possible solutions to the crime in Clue. But, in real life, if you're not careful, you'll confront so many choices your head will spin."

"Then the game plays you," replies the Gnome, contentedly.

"Point and match," I reply.

Eric again. "Every decision should advance you towards your goal, or at least, minimize setbacks."

I ponder the Gnome's three lessons. Clue, like all great board games, offers simple truths if you are receptive.

The Gnome studies the hands on the grandfather clock. "Phil, there's one more place connected to Clue that we must visit."

WADDINGTON'S PRINTING WORKS
Wakefield Road, Leeds 10, England

WHERE WADDINGTON'S PLAYING CARDS AND GAMES ARE MADE

On our way out, Eric gestures towards the pictures handing on the wall. They include an official portrait of Norman Watson, one of the imposing Waddington "Printing Works" on Wakefield Road in Leeds, and several picturing other editions of Clue and Cluedo. "Over two hundred million copies sold by now," Eric informs us. "Loads of improved versions between 1949 and the present. An even bigger game named Clue Master Detective. But the original is still my favorite."

The final photo is of Anthony Pratt in elder age, sitting at a table and playing his brainchild. I discern a note of unhappiness in his bespectacled eyes. And what of this man, Anthony Pratt, this gifted genius who defied war, created a great game, got it published, and gave the game-playing world an eternal gift?

We're off in a taxi once more, thirteen miles southwest, to a quiet cemetery in Bromsgrove. The Gnome leads me to a simple tombstone upon which is inscribed:

In
Loving Memory of
A very dear father
Born 10 August 1903
Died 9 April 1994
INVENTOR OF 'CLUEDO'
Sadly Missed

"Did Pratt apply the wisdom he imbued in Cluedo?" I ask the Gnome.

The Gnome shakes his head. "Sadly, no. In 1953, he accepted a buyout of his international royalties, worth about two hundred thousand dollars today—a fraction of what Clue's international sales would have earned him. And he made an even bigger mistake. Because of his compulsion to patent his game, he agreed to limit his royalties to the life of the patent, and thus his royalties ceased in 1967."

Pratt, apparently, didn't see the irrelevance of this. His game was also granted a copyright; a copyright endures far longer. More importantly, the *idea* for Cluedo, which is really what he gave Waddingtons, endures forever. Pratt did not need to limit his payment "term."

The Gnome says softly, "Anthony Pratt and wife Elva watched as bystanders while Clue's success mounted throughout the remainder of their lives."

"Did Anthony ever invent another game?"

"Not that I know of. Certainly, none that were published. He went back to his office career and reclaimed anonymity. His wife died in 1990 and he, as we see on his stone, in 1994."

I ponder the inscription requested by Pratt's son: "Sadly Missed."

The Gnome laments, "Must have been tough for him. A slow twilight. Fortunately, no other inventor we seek made a similar mistake."

"Who's next?" I ask. "More importantly, What's the big picture? Don't lead me in the dark. Shine a light."

The Gnome contemplates, rubs his beard, and accepts my plea. His eyes twinkle, devilishly so. "We've only just begun," he lilts, to the tune of the same name. "If you are up for it...if you are game...a long journey lies ahead. With many stops. I promise you won't forget any of them, or the lessons that await."

We dine in style that night. In the morning, after a hearty English breakfast (I do love bangers), we fly back to Boston. Curiously, the Gnome tells me our next goal is Philadelphia.

Hmm.

CHAPTER TWO

SOUP AND OILCLOTH

Our train is about to cross the Delaware River. We began our trip five hours ago onboard a commuter rail in Salem, Massachusetts (where the Parker Brothers game factory stood proudly for over a century), then switched to Amtrak's Acela at Boston's South Station. We could have flown directly to Philadelphia, but the Gnome wants me in a 1930s frame of mind, when a passenger train was to transportation as Babe Ruth was to baseball. Both were kings. Besides, he notes, "There are four trains on the Monopoly board. No airplanes."

We rent a car at 30th Street Station and he drives northwest towards Germantown Avenue. The trolley tracks that once scarred its surface have been paved over. I know where the Gnome is taking me. I have been here before. So why must I go back to Westview Avenue and the home where Charles Brace Darrow and his family once lived? After all, I am already as connected to the Monopoly game as anyone, having written three books with its name in the title, and a fourth (a history of games-maker Parker Brothers) that featured it.

The Gnome holds his consul. "When you look around today, it is difficult to realize just how hard hit was Philadelphia by the Depression. In 1933, real unemployment was thirty percent. Imagine, on every third stoop along this street, we see a man sitting idly. Imagine you have no job, no income, no prospects. Imagine the humiliation of being compelled to stand in line for soup every day."

Back then, federal relief was minimal. Half the country's population lived in cities and could not produce its own food. Charities and churches tried to plug the gap. To receive aid in downtown Philly, you shuffled "on the line" until you reached a table where a caring soul ladled you a bowl of potato and cabbage soup (maybe with some meat) and offered you a hunk of bread. Other lines promised coffee and a doughnut.

Times were clearly chaotic, not due to conflict, but to a disorder of economics. The wind had been knocked out of capitalism by a business downturn, a gaping downdraft in the stock market (self-inflicted due to the indiscriminate use of margin loans for stock purchases), and a "tell the foreigners to stuff it" tariff war. Worse yet, nobody knew how long this malaise would last. (All crystal balls went cloudy, it seems.)

Charles Darrow was desperately trying to avoid the "line." He had been a salesman of steam radiators, or perhaps a radiator repairman, or both. His brick two-story home was a pleasant reminder of his "everyman" success. But now, Darrow's regular paycheck was a memory. His wife, Esther, had a small income as a seamstress; otherwise, the money had stopped. Things tend to go bad quickly when that happens. Darrow tried to improvise by hiring himself out as a handyman. Relying on innate cleverness, he made wood puzzles and devised novelties like an improved cribbage scoring pad. He sustained none of these. Then Lady Chance "arranged' an unexpected encounter with a couple named Charles and Olive Todd. Darrow's wife, Esther, and Charles Todd had gone to school together. Their reunion proved a happy occasion. The Todds invited the Darrows to dinner. They agreed to get together again, and on that occasion, they invited the Darrows to play a handmade game.

Fast forward. Darrow, taken by this game, has spent time with the Todds to learn it correctly. Charles Todd has complied and provided a few typed copies of its rules—sketchy at best. Darrow learns that the game is unpublished. Many people have made their own copies; it is traditional to give yours a flavor incorporating the local surroundings.

The game's chain was long and loose. The Todds were introduced to the game by friends living in Atlantic City, a resort in New Jersey known as the "World's Playground." In turn, these friends had come upon it from a school principal newly arrived from Indianapolis.

Unlike most others, the Todds did not change the property names on their board, choosing to retain its Atlantic City identity (although they did misspell "Marven Gardens" and shortened the name of a railroad—actually, a bus company—to the "Short Line). Darrow then sets about making his own version. But he does not "torture" cardboard, as had Anthony Pratt, to fashion his game board. No, his first copy of the Monopoly game is laid out on a large circular oilcloth.

Oilcoth. I remember my mother protected our dining table with a tablecloth made out of oilcloth—it was yellow and decorated with white flowers. So what is oilcloth? I look it up. It's a linen cloth coated with boiled linseed oil to make it waterproof. It is slightly stiff. Good for rain gear, good for table covers. Unprinted, it is pale beige in color. Ideal for Darrow's purpose.

Courtesy of the Strong, Rochester, NY

Darrow keeps the Atlantic City names intact, including Todd's alterations. While Todd's game is devoid of artwork, Darrow draws bold symbols on several spaces. And whereas the Todd game featured small colored triangles in the lower left corners of its property spaces, Darrow replaces these with bolder, more obvious "color bars" along the top of the properties.

Store-bought money is used for the game's currency. Chunky wood moldings are cut into small pieces to become houses and hotels. Deeds and cards are cut from thin cardboard sheets after being typed by hand. Darrow rummages for household objects, like a penny and a thimble, to serve as playing pieces.

Charles Brace Darrow, circa 1955

It's hot and humid in Philly, like most summer days. As I mop my brow, the Gnome's eyes go mystical on me. His voice becomes subdued. "I see a lot of people along this street, mainly men aimlessly walking the sidewalks. But not Darrow. Darrow is sheltered in the shade of his little front porch, laying out a Monopoly board on a card table. He is a husky man with a round face, long ears, and bespectacled eyes. He is about to play his game with two young girls—his niece, Mary, and her friend, Mary Jean. They are talking about tokens. The girls each remove a charm from their wrist bracelets. Esther has come out carrying a glass pitcher filled with iced tea. She sets it on a side table and pours four glasses."

There are so many stories about the origin of the playing pieces for Monopoly. My favorite is about the tokens. The tiny metal "charms" ultimately included in the game were likely inspired by Darrow's niece and her friend. "What else of the game do you see?" I ask the Games Gnome. He tells me: a square oilcloth board (not Darrow's original round version) neatly lined and painted, plus the typical Darrow components.

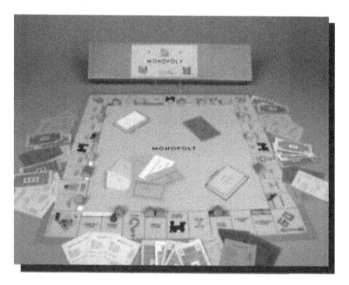

Courtesy of the Strong. Rochester, NY

Weeks have elapsed since crossing paths with the Todds. Darrow is laboriously making bespoke copies of the game for enthused friends and charging four dollars each. He had located a supply of necktie boxes (as used by department stores to house their supplies) and packs a rolled-up oilcloth and a complete set of playing components inside of each.

Eventually, he will seek out a printer to print the black lines and text copy on his oilcloths and print the deeds on colored cardboard. The following year, 1934, further emboldened, he obtains an order from the prestigious John Wanamaker Department Store in downtown Philadelphia (famous for the pipe organ in its lobby). Oilcoth gives way to tortured cardboard; the tie box is discarded in favor of custom boxes big enough to house a folded board. In-between, Darrow has become good friends with a newly arrived artist in his neighborhood, Franklin Alexander, who draws comic strips under the pen name F.O. Alexander. Using Darrow's original art as a guide, Alexander styles the game and develops arresting illustrations for its box's otherwise white cover. He does this as a favor, without charge.

Monopoly becomes a quick success at Wanamaker's. Darrow orders another five hundred copies to meet holiday demand for this one store. The buyer, a Mister MacDonald—who has befriended Darrow—is pleased, but he does not favor the large white box and its three-dollar price tag (more than fifty in today's dollars). He suggests, beginning the following year, that Darrow offer a small utensil box and a separate board, lower the price accordingly, and thereby match how the "big boys" (à la Parker Brothers) merchandise their most popular games.

Darrow begins to do a bit of trade advertising. Monopoly is then picked up by the major toy chain FAO Schwarz. One of those who would buy a copy in an FAO store is a lady named Helen Coolidge. She is a childhood friend of Sally Barton, daughter of George Parker—founder of Parker Brothers. Sally is married to Robert Barton who is now running the firm. After Helen tells Sally "It's quite a game. It's named Monopoly," Sally tells Robert and soon thereafter, Robert meets with Charles.

Darrow now owns a whopping 7,500 copies of his new "black box" edition. He receives more orders from John Wanamaker, and other accounts have begun to "nibble." But Darrow is realizing there is much more to running a game *business* than just making a game (i.e., mainly headaches). He is delighted to sell his inventory and accept a royalty on future sales by Parker Brothers.

Thirty-some years after Elizabeth Magie, a lady living outside of Washington, D.C., patented a politically-motivated game entitled "The Landlord's Game," its metamorphic journey across college campuses and through the hands of a couple of lesser entrepreneurs was completed. Darrow's expression of the game—his copyrighted design—is the one America will go nuts over.

Parker Brothers is the nation's best-known game company at this time. The fifty-year old firm has national distribution but badly needs a hit to keep afloat. Robert Barton puts all his firm's chips behind Monopoly. His bet pays off. Eighteen months later, over two million sets have been sold. Sales ebb in the late 1930s, but they recover when Parker begins supplying copies for the armed forces during World War II. By 1952, sales once again surpass a million copies annually and never look back. Eventually, hundreds of millions will be sold globally.

These are the highlights, of course. The history of Monopoly is rich and multi-layered. It was even used to smuggle escape tools to allied prisoners in World War II. The Gnome embraces history, but this is not his passion today. So what is his point? When he disengages from 1935 and returns to the present, it sharpens like a pencil.

"Darrow was an inevitability," the Gnome says. "You can think of him as a hero or a devil, depending on whose side you are on, but he was bound to come along, just like the sun after a storm. Why? Because even our most distant ancestors loved real estate and were willing to kill for it, according to the busted bones anthropologists have studied. This powerful, primordial desire endures. It was certain to one day spark a 'can't-miss' game."

"By somebody, somewhere."

"I am saying that chance assured that—if not a Charles Darrow—then a Manny, Moe, or Jack…or a Jane. Darrow happened to be the person who crossed the game's Rubicon. Others had made tepid tries or cowered. He didn't. Applause. As a result, Monopoly was offered up to the crowd."

Crowd? Did the Gnome say the word crowd? "Crowds can be rowdy," I reply.

"Oh, how true. The crowd does not think rationally as, supposedly, does an individual. But after chaos causes a game's inception and chance sustained it, every great one needs a crowd to give it a shot at immortality."

I gather the Gnome means that, initially, when only a few individuals play a game here and there, there is no conviction to compel the multitude to rush out to buy the "new game in town." To accomplish this, reason must be overcome.

The Gnome is on the move. "Let us depart Westview Avenue and head to Center City."

Downtown, a few miles away on Walnut Street near the Delaware River, stands Bookbinder's Restaurant. A city landmark since the late 1800s, it endured bankruptcy and, after many fits and starts, has reopened to (hopefully) regain its former glory.

It was here, all those years go, that I first learned about cardboard, and the proper way to "torture" (alter) it to make boxes and game boards. My teacher was Joe Milestone, the owner of the Acme Paper Box Company in North Philly. "Do you know about osmosis?" was his first question. I told him sure, college chemistry and all. "Well, osmosis is why the glue sinks into cardboard to fasten the paper sheet we wrap around it in order to make your game boxes." Joe, the ever-thoughtful professor, felt compelled to describe the process of making cardboard itself. Now, most of us have about as much curiosity about this topic as we do about how rocks turn into sand. But Joe could make it fascinating. Trees, logs, wood pulp, chemicals, water, screening, pressing, drying with heat rollers, Anne Brontë (she coined the word "cardboard" in a novel back in 1848), and the Kellogg Brothers (first to use cardboard to box their cornflakes in 1906). Joe went on to describe how sheets of cardboard are tortured to make boxes: sliced, die-cut, scored, bent, stayed (corners taped), glued, wrapped with paper, collated, and bundled. Likewise, game boards are sliced, die-cut, taped, glued, and wrapped top and bottom—just like a book cover—and oh, isn't it fascinating that we're dining in a restaurant named Bookbinders?

I knew that Joe invited only his most important clients to the prestigious Bookbinders. *So why me?* "To use your term, Phil," Joe said with a kindly smile, "I believe you are destined to torture a great deal of cardboard during your career." He added with mild probation, "You understand that I prefer the term 'fabricate.' It is more scientific."

I have not been inside Bookbinders since, Joe having passed on. Its brick building neighborhood still evokes Colonial times. The restaurant has a dark green facade and the "Bookbinders" name is emblazoned on each side of a portico. Under the portico, its main doors project from a windowed red enclosure that reminds one of a double-sized London phone booth. Inside, one notices richly paneled wood and glassy multi-pane windows; it could well be a London club. We are led to a private room adorned with portraits of past presidents. A lady is glaring at us, seated at a game table upon whose surface is spread a Monopoly game. (What else should I expect?)

I am introduced to Doctor Marion Nicé. She is of French origin; her last name is pronounced "Knee-say." Raised from a young age in America, there is only a subtle hint of an accent. She is quite stylish, somewhere in her forties, and while I detect an air of conceit, she is very pleasant to the eye. Her full lips are expressive; her dark green eyes are almost the same shade as the facade of Bookbinders. Doctor Nicé is a clinical physician turned psychologist.

The Gnome sets the stage. "As you well know, Phil, most people think games are mere playthings. They are not curious about their history. However, when a new hit game suddenly pops out of nowhere and becomes part of the landscape, everyone abruptly accepts it, seemingly at once. It doesn't seem to matter what they were thinking beforehand. That's the crowd talking."

Doctor Nicé agrees. "But of course. Now let us play."

We pick tokens. I take the Cannon; it is easy to lift with one's fingers. She selects the cute Scotty; the Gnome takes the Racecar (the game's most popular token). We order drinks and a house special—seafood finger sandwiches. We roll; she will move first.

"I am a very accomplished Monopoly player," she proclaims. "By the way, I have read your books." Doctor Nicé lands on Reading Railroad—reminding us that it is pronounced "REDing," not "Reeding"—and buys it. "Your friend has invited me here not only to demonstrate my prowess over the board, but to tell you my social theory of Monopoly. A topic you have not written about."

While I have I described Monopoly's impact on culture, Doctor Nicé claims to have a different angle up the sleeve of her silk blouse.

"She has a distant relative," the Gnome explains. "A famous man in his time and beyond."

"My great-great-great uncle was a physician, named Le Bon. Gustave Le Bon." (I think to myself: Gus the Good.) "He wrote a book that developed quite a following, *Psychologie des Foules*—better known as The Psychology of the Crowd, or simply The Crowd. His theories became the basis for all the research that followed. They apply to games, and especially the one we are playing, Monopoly. For what good is a game if no one knows of it?" She echoes the Gnome's point, "It takes a crowd to make a game."

She explains which conclusions arrived at by her "triple great" uncle are hereby relevant. "Le Bon does not define the crowd as a mob. A crowd is simply many, many people, together or isolated, it doesn't matter. But these people do act differently when they join a crowd. They may be, individually, quite rational. But put them together and they transform into a collective crowd wherein they feel, think, and act *much* differently."

While she is speaking, the game is progressing. We each have several properties. I pick up two of the Yellow properties. With luck, I'll get the third and then build houses. Yes!

"Tell Phil about the appeal of the crowd," the Gnome urges.

"A crowd, Gustave wrote, creates a sense of invincible power that causes the individuals to yield to it. The sentiment of responsibility disappears entirely. Once that happens, we get the contagion.

"Contagion is when everyone suddenly feels the same about something. Then all become vulnerable because of suggestibility. As my dear ancestor once said, 'Suggestibility is the state of fascination in which the hypnotized individual finds himself in the hands of the hypnotizer.' By now, his or her ability to reason is far below the level of an individual. Sanity has become absent."

I think of Carl Jung's take on this: "*The bigger the crowd, the more negligible the individual.*" I realize the "crowd" that he and Gustave Le Bon are speaking of sounds nothing like something any of us would want to join, until—without thinking—we do.

She continues, "In order for anything, like a game, to become popular, many people need to suspend logic and join the crowd. I tell you about Monopoly. Parker Brothers—like any company that caters to the whims of the public—is not a maker of games. It is a *maker of crowds.* If it does not make crowds, it fails and will no longer be able to make games."

The evidence supports her. Parker enjoyed a reasonable success with Monopoly during the balance of 1935. But in 1936, the game's first full year with Parker, all logic became suspended. The "crowd" formed immediately after New Year's Day. Those who had played Monopoly with friends during the holidays decided they had to have their own copies. They in turn played it with *their* friends, and the crowd grew. Friends played with more friends and the crowd mushroomed. Individuals in all parts of the United States were, unknowingly, thinking alike. Only a month or two earlier, the Monopoly game would have engendered a blank stare from most folks; now its mere mention stirred a universal craving. *I must have it.* (Lack of money, apparently, was not a deterrent—Depression be damned.)

The Gnome speaks as a learned scholar. "There were thirty-one million households in the United States in 1935. The average family earned fifteen hundred dollars. Unemployment was still over twenty percent. So only twenty-five million households had an income. Between 1935 and 1936, more than two million sets of Monopoly were sold. That means one per twelve working households. Each paid about three dollars for a set. That's the equivalent of fifty dollars today. Is that not astounding? I mean, Monopoly today retails for maybe fifteen dollars. Yet back then, with much less money in hand, folks were willing to pay three times as much!"

I don't question the Gnome's facts. He has an airtight memory, and they confirm my research.

Doctor Nicé says, "Once again, proof of crowd mentality. If you are a laborer earning thirty dollars per week, how do you justify spending fully ten percent of that on—as you call it, Philip—a box of tortured cardboard?"

"Because the excitement has swept you up," I reply.

"And who do you become?"

"A member of the crowd."

"Certainement."

"Crowd mentality even affects the play of the game itself," the Gnome notes. Marion smiles.

"Philip, Monopoly is also unique because during its play, a crowd must form or, if resisted, the individuals will be swiftly bankrupted," she says.

Having rolled doubles, Doctor Nicé picks up the dice and rolls again, draws a Chance card and advances to Illinois Avenue. Not only does she already own three railroads, Illinois completes her set of three Reds. "As you can see, gentlemen, I have enough cash to buy seven houses. I shall do so. Now, how do you respond?"

The Gnome and I *must* trade with each other in order to complete our color groups or her Reds will likely impoverish us. I have my two Yellows, and the Gnome owns the third, Atlantic Avenue. I happen to own two Light Blues to his one. We must trade. Neither of us wants to do so. But we do.

Neither gains an advantage over the other and the particulars are rather bloody. But at least we each own a group to compete with Doctor Nicé and her threatening Reds.

When the trade dust settles, she says, rather smugly, "You have just demonstrated crowd thinking within the game. Whereas formerly you were not interested in trading, hoping to land on and acquire properties to improve your position, suddenly you were hypnotized and could think of nothing but trading. And at virtually any price." She adds, "Of course, if we had two or three other desperate players in the game, the crowd would have been bigger, noisier, and even more irrational."

Doctor Nicé is not so nice when it comes to sportsmanship.

"I know your secrets, Philip. Having read your book, I understand the Oranges and Reds to be the best groups, that three houses is infinitely superior to owning two houses per property, and that the Railroads provide the cash to fund their construction." Her smile has a hint of triumph when she concludes with, "You cannot win; you know that, yes?"

Well, no. I don't know that. I mean, at the moment she is favored to win, but there is much luck in Monopoly, and if it goes my way…I draw a Chance card: "Advance to Illinois Avenue." Oops. I must tear down my houses on the Yellows to pay the rent. My odds of winning are now about as great as driving from here to Cleveland without hitting a red light.

"I don't enjoy playing Monopoly," the Gnome confesses after Doctor Nicé bankrupts him. He surrenders his Light Blues to her. "But I am able to profit from the pearls of wisdom imparted by this immensely influential game."

"Such as?" Doctor Nicé asks, as she scoops us the Gnome's other meager holdings.

"Many Gnomes are known to accumulate riches. I have applied the tenets of Monopoly to secure mine. For example: to anticipate the unexpected, don't fight it, profit from it. Also, it is best to diversify one's investments; there is too much risk putting everything in one basket, be it a mutual fund or a stock you happen to fall in love with. Oh, by the way, you may love an investment but remember that investment does not know you own it, and it is incapable of returning your affection."

"Anything else?" I ask. Having written an entire book on Monopoly's lessons, I prefer to hear the Gnome drill further.

"Don't borrow unless you must or unless you anticipate a high return for the risk involved. Pay off your most costly debts first. Only invest when you are calm and rational; don't become part of a crowd. Doctor Nicé knows what she is talking about here. Oh, and since we often get sideswiped by bad luck, you should take swift advantage of good luck when it happens. Don't squander it on a party. Invest it." *Touché,* I think to myself.

I roll and land on Pennsylvania Railroad. Most unfortunate. I can't come up with one hundred dollars to pay Doctor Nicé without mortgaging a Yellow property. I resign as graciously as I can. I know a "secret" from experience. In Monopoly, you often fare better—in this game and the next—if you present yourself as a player the others won't mind losing to. (Doctor Nicé seems not to have acquired this insight.) Why is this important? In real life, opportunities often come your way, thanks to the recommendation of others. The more people who find you to be reasonable, the more opportunities you'll get. Once I figured this out, it worked innumerable times for me and advanced my career.

We make our good-byes. Doctor Nicé pays the bill. "To the victors go the spoils and the check," she says, rather pleasantly.

The Gnome whisks us back to 30th Street Station and, two hours later, we are standing on the boardwalk in Atlantic City, invigorated by mild ocean air, looking down on a plaque opposite Park Place honoring Charles Darrow.

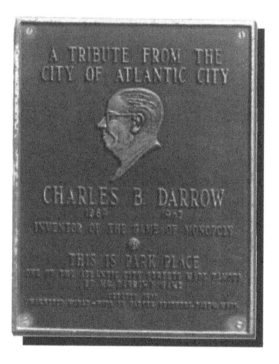

I remark to the Gnome, "If you're going to pay homage to Monopoly on a plaque, technically, it should honor Parker Brothers, not Darrow."

"People don't connect with companies like they do with other people," the Gnome retorts. "Darrow, right or wrong, represents the aspiration of many who dream of rising above and making it big."

"Ah, that would be a Crowd talking."

Chapter Three

MAN OF LETTERS

We're in a cab leaving LaGuardia Airport heading south on a muggy summer's day, a week later. The Gnome is mum about our destination, but I begin to suspect he is taking me back to where I once lived with my wife and firstborn son: in Elmhurst, Queens—a couple of miles from here.

I'm wrong. Our trip ends abruptly on 35th Avenue, the main thoroughfare in Jackson Heights. As the Gnome pays the fare, I find myself gazing at long rows of six-story brick apartment buildings. "Look at the sign, Phil!" The Gnome is pointing to the corner street sign, which reads, rather oddly…

35 $T_1 H_4 \ A_1 V_4 E_1 N_1 U_1 E_1$

Scrabble. The Gnome turns right and begins walking with purpose. "Follow me. Alfred Butts lived on this street." We amble through a blend of South Americans, Latinos, and Asians on the sidewalk. The neighborhood has evolved significantly since the years when I lived "next door."

"We're going up to his old haunts. I got permission from the current tenant." The Gnome presses a buzzer and says a few words in Spanish. I find myself on his heels, hiking up four flights of stairs observing that his shoes have gold buckles. He knocks, and a dark-skinned lady wearing an apron admits us to her small apartment. She's doing dishes. The Gnome has a gift for her: a glittering brooch; she accepts it with a warm smile.

The Games Gnome turns his attention to the kitchen table upon which sits a red plate with golden *sopa paraguaya*, as the lady calls her cornbread. She urges us to try some as she rushes to pour coffee. But the Gnome is no longer with us. I watch, enthralled. He has transformed; he speaks softly, "His table, of course, is not this modern one. It's wooden, and Alfie's sitting there, this little man, pouring over a story page in the *Saturday Evening Post*, meticulously counting how many times each letter of the alphabet appears. Alfred Mosher Butts is a plain man, bookish. The type you wouldn't notice in a crowd. Bald head, glasses, bemused expression. But he seems happy with his preoccupation, like a bean counter in love with his figures. Compulsive, determined, consumed. There's a hand-made game on the table. It consists of wood racks made out of moldings, like Darrow's houses and hotel, and lots of letter tiles cut from plywood. Glued to their surfaces is linen cloth with hand-drawn letters and numbers inked on them. Oh, wait…"

"Something happening?"

"Indeed. Alfie just swept the letter tiles toward himself and appears to be sorting them. Seems he's trying to decide how many to include for his next play session." The Gnome pauses. "He just counted out a hundred and ten…wait, he picks out ten and dumps them into a bowl. He's down to one hundred. Oops. Seems he's got too many 'Es.' He discards two and now he's got thirteen of them. Hold the phone…he doesn't like thirteen, he settles for twelve. Now he digs in the bowl and comes up with an 'R' and an 'N.' He's smiling. There he goes again, this time maneuvering ten 'A' tiles. Nah. Too many, apparently. One is tossed into the bowl. He takes a moment to spill some Planter's peanuts from a bag and scoops them into his mouth. Oh dear, he just ate the extra 'A.' He spits it out with a look of disgust, like a child protesting his spinach. Now he mutters something about having two 'Ks' so he could spell 'kink.' But then he slides over a 'J' and asks it what it thinks about having two 'K's'…" the Gnome pauses again momentarily "…and apparently the 'J' says no."

"He talks to his letter tiles?"

"Like I said, he's compulsive. The extra 'K' is gone. Butts is now writing furiously."

"What's all that about?"

"Alfie is recording the letter distribution and dating it, September twenty-six, 1933."

"You're back in the chaos of the Depression, in the same year Darrow made his Monopoly game and board by hand."

"Can't be helped."

"What about the game's board?"

"There is no game board. At least not yet."

"Are we talking about Scrabble, then?" I ask.

"Not by name. Butts has not got the full game as we know it, and he has not come up with the right name for his invention, which is still rudimentary. His notebook is titled 'Lexiko' and it is filled with page after page after page of notes pertaining to letter frequency. Do you know why?"

"What?" I am still chewing on the name "Lexiko," unconsciously thinking of a laxative. "Oh, you just told me. He's experimenting, trying to figure out how many tiles of each letter to include in his game. There are probably no standard references to consult about letter usage back then." This seems likely to me because I had to do something similar while working on letter distribution to include in "Big Boggle" during my time at Parker Brothers.

"His notebook also contains tables of possible scoring values for each letter. He knows the rarer the letter tile in his game, the more it should be worth. But he doesn't seem to have fixed these as yet."

"I wonder how long it took him to get it right."

The Gnome's head rolls involuntarily; he drops into a deep catatonic state—his eyes unblinking, his lips rigid. The lady of the house is still trying to interest him in coffee; I suggest she put his cup on the counter; I thank her for mine; powerful stuff, but appealing.

Several minutes later, the Gnome is again with us. *What just happened?* The dark coffee is tepid enough for him to swig. Then we make our goodbyes.

Sitting in an aromatic café a few blocks away, the Gnome tells me the tale of Alfred Butts, and what hypnotized him for so long while in the apartment where this humble genius crafted what became Scrabble.

Alfred Butts, like Charles Darrow, had lost his job during the Depression. The thirty-two-year-old had been an architect. Like Darrow, he tried a few ventures (writing, painting, illustrating) with only limited success. Unlike Darrow, he found another job, part-time, as a statistician at a welfare agency. With abundant free time, he decided to create a game in an effort to make up the shortfall in his income. Butts, meticulous in all his pursuits, was a great record-keeper and this aided him after he decided on creating a word formation game. He was driven to perfect the selection of letter tiles in his game to permit the maximum amount of English language words to be spelled.

"The reason I zoned out for so long," the Gnome explains while seasoning his green salad, "is because I had to visualize Butts' long journey. He did not go from his Lexiko game to what became Scrabble in a flash. In fact, it took him five years before he even came up with the idea of adding a game board. And when he did, he rechristened his game Criss-Cross Words."

"Clearly, the imprint of Scrabble is there. The board I saw was fifteen spaces by fifteen spaces. There were premium squares for bonus letter and word scores; there was symmetry in their locations and values, and a central start space marked with a 'star.' These were the result of half a decade of dedicated experimenting by Alfred Butts. Yet we take his labored conclusions as self-evident today. Even the size of the board was the result of much experimenting. Butts tried boards with fourteen, sixteen, and seventeen spaces along each side. He laid out the premium squares in odd patterns. He put the Start space in the corners or off-center. In the end, he settled upon a gridded pattern quite pleasing to the eye. Don't you think?"

I agree, then ask, "Did he make multiple copies of his two games, or simply a prototype?"

"Multiple, just like Darrow, in an attempt to make some money. He cobbled his sets by hand in his living room. packing them in whatever boxes he could get his hands on. Ironically, just about the time he introduced Criss-Cross Words, his former employer rehired him. That took pressure off his need to sell games to stay afloat. He gradually lost interest. Nine years later, in 1947, he was about to give up."

"What happened?" I ask. The Gnome tells me to finish my lunch; we're going for a ride.

Thanks to Uber and a couple of hours' time, we drive to Newtown, Connecticut, and amble along a residential street until the Gnome says, "Pull over." He points out a stately colonial home. "James Brunot lived there when he turned Alfred's game into Scrabble."

So who was James Brunot? The Gnome explains that Brunot was a director at a New York welfare agency when he approached Alfred Butts in 1947 about taking over production of Criss-Cross Words. Seems Brunot was tired of his long commute from Newtown to New York City and was looking for a product he could make and sell from home. Brunot was forty-five, three years younger than Butts. By pure chance, much as Darrow happened upon Monopoly, Brunot ran into an acquaintance—a social worker who happened to have tested Criss-Cross Words. He showed his copy to Brunot, who realized that with some improvements, making this game professionally could be a profitable venture. Butts was more than happy to accept his offer.

Brunot spiffed up the colors on the game board, tweaked five premium spaces and came up with the name we all know: "Scrabble." He liked it because it sounded like "scramble" and its definition "to scratch or grope around" fit. Plus, his attorneys said it was "clear" and could be trademarked.

They settle on one hundred tiles per set. While the final distribution of letters is not perfect—it's rather impossible to match actual letter usage with only a hundred tiles—Butts' final selection is ideal for a word game. The most rarely used letters (j, k, q, x, z) only appear once, while the prolific vowels abound. All that compilation of newspaper and magazine pages pays a nice dividend. I wonder how many other people would have had the patience to persist with analysis this tedious. Of course, today, we have computers; Butts only had paper and a pencil.

Brunot gave his company the bland name of "The Production and Marketing Corporation." An abandoned schoolhouse served as its "factory" and its picture appeared on the company's sales brochure. Even though Brunot was a savvy businessman, he was not an instinctive marketer and relied on word-of-mouth and a few small advertisements to generate sales, which came in dribs and drabs. It took him five agonizing years to increase sales to ten thousand copies per year. By then, Brunot was reaching the end of his enthusiasm for the game. And then magic occurred.

That summer, after he and his wife returned from a vacation in Kentucky he found orders waiting for 2,500 sets. What? A fluke? No. The following week, three thousand more sets were ordered. And it was straight up from there.

So how did this miracle occur? Chance, once again. It seems the chairman of Macy's Department Store, Jack Straus, had stayed an extra day on his vacation in the Hamptons on Long Island and had reluctantly accepted a dinner invite from friends vacationing nearby. They had Scrabble with them.

Would he like to try playing it? "Why not?" Strauss replied. He liked it immensely but was miffed when he got back to work and learned his prestigious store did not carry this "fashionable" game. He fixed that. When his competitors learned Macy's was doing nice business with Scrabble, they all had to order it. Strauss had induced a crowd.

Brunot now scrambled ("scrabbled"?) to keep up with demand. His firm moved into the facility of an old woodworking company, outsourced much of the game's components, and licensed a cheaper cardboard version but still could not keep up with demand. Major publications were writing adoring columns about Scrabble and how it had supplanted Canasta as the pastime of the upper crust and sophisticated. Celebrities were photographed playing it. Demand quickly exceeded ten thousand sets a week. In 1953 alone, over a million total sets were sold. Shortages drove demand even higher.

"The crowd had mushroomed," the Gnome opines. "It had a mind of its own, and all it wanted was Scrabble and more Scrabble." The year 1954 became insane; almost four million sets were sold. The rush calmed down thereafter, but just like Monopoly's sales, they eventually bounced back to around a million copies a year and have flourished ever since."

Years before, and thanks to a coincidence, Alfred Butts had learned of the game maker Selchow & Righter, located in Brooklyn. He ordered some three hundred game boards from the firm and they obliged. he enthusiastically recommended the firm to Brunot during the production crunch. S&R came through and Brunot sold out to the firm in the late 1960s and retired comfortably, as did Butts. (We'll hear more about "S&R" in another chapter.)

I want to ask the Gnome how the two men shared the revenue of Scrabble, but he's studying a map. We have another stop to make. He drives west to Danbury, Connecticut. Along the way, he opens up a bit about his past.

"My mother loved to played Scrabble when I was growing up. I can see her playing with her friends, the mountains visible through our kitchen window. While she liked to play four-player games, she thought Scrabble was best for two. She taught me how to play as soon as I could grasp it. And we always played head-to-head."

"Why isn't Scrabble as good with three or four players?"

"For one thing, the player who goes first affects your fate. He or she might open up great scoring opportunities, but if you go fourth, these opportunities often disappear by the time it is your turn."

"That's a criticism of many multi-player strategy games."

"I know. Scrabble is also a game where many use 'house rules' without even knowing it. Take my friend, Tiel. He never hesitates to put down a word he believes to be real. Why? Because at his place, even if his opponent challenges, there is no penalty. You just take the word back and try again. That is no fun."

I build on this. "I've seen serious players purposely lay down low-scoring fake words to get rid of unwanted letters. There are so many obscure two and three-letter words. They know you might not call their bluff. If you challenge and are wrong, you *lose* a turn."

The Gnome grimaces; he is about to make a point from experience. "There's nothing more annoying than an opponent who, after the game ends, points out all the fake words he slipped by you. Makes me utter some words that are not in the

Scrabble dictionary. And every once in a while, one of these players throws in a really obscure word hoping you *will* challenge and lose your turn."

I tell the Gnome, "I once asked a passionate Scrabble player, Daniel Ducoff, a vice dean at my alma mater, CWRU, how he handles challenging. Daniel is, as you might imagine, intelligent, respected, and erudite—I mean he is a one step from being a dean. His advice was equally illuminating: I grab this person by the collar and yell, 'Are you messing with me?'"

"Seriously?"

"No. Daniel actually said, 'It depends on how many points are at stake and if the word in question blocks my progress. If it's not worth much, why bother? If it's a game-changer, I will certainly challenge.' Then Daniel offered more insight into the merits of Scrabble. 'My wife, Ronni, credits Scrabble with teaching her, while still young, the importance of reading opponents' body language and sizing up their vocabulary proficiency before deciding to challenge. She is now a prosecutor and uses her skill to decide when to challenge—and when not to challenge—her legal opponent. Real-life stakes.'"

The Gnome remarks, offhandedly, "My friends are rather like Daniel and Ronni. And we are about to meet them." We pull into a tree-lined driveway and park next to a nicely-restored clapboard home amidst a flowering yard and goldfish pond.

Suzanne and Gerald Sweeney greet us at the painted door. ("Call me Suzie, with a 'z.' He prefers Gerald.") Suzi could pass for a fortyish Joyce DeWitt (remember her from "Three's Company"?) thanks to her curly dark hair and bright-eyed expression. He is a *doublegange*r for a middle-aged James Coburn: large-jawed, wiry, prematurely gray.

Their home is lovely, the snacks are delicious, and their "game den" is handsomely lined with bookshelves. I glance at a few titles; they are technical, covering such fun topics as cryptanalysis, medical terminology, proofreading, and computer jargon. It comes as no surprise to learn "Suzie" is a former editor of a medical journal and is now a freelance journalist. Gerald once worked for the NSA as a code breaker and is now writing manuals for software firms. In other "words," they are word junkies. Naturally, they can't wait to get out the board.

Suzie's dip in the bag yields a "Q," assuring she will go first. She tries to be reassuring. I note that she draws out certain words, as if they're in need of added emphasis. "Now don't take offense, but of c-o-u-r-s-e, we will win, but I don't believe our friend the Gnome would have it any o-t-h-e-r way!"

The Gnome shrugs; he's bemused. "They never lose. But that's not why we are here. They have a theory. Wait 'til you hear it, Phil."

On the first play, Suzie lays down ZORINOS. *What?* "It's the fur of a skunk," she explains, cheerily recording a score of eighty-four points (including the fifty bonus points for a "bingo"—playing all seven tiles on her rack). I manage PETRIE, which unfortunately, sets up Gerald to lay down his own intersecting bingo: VARIEDLY (yes, it is a word) which scores several dozen points.

After a while, I begin to wonder if these two will set some kind of scoring record. And I can't help but notice they have this habit of closing their eyes, exhaling and instantly relaxing, whenever the Gnome or I ponder our next word.

No matter. The Gnome eventually persuades them to suspend play and tell us the lessons imparted by Scrabble (I know one, for sure: don't play with word fanatics like these two). "Phil, Gerald has developed a theory, as I mentioned. He calls it the Power Web. Listen up."

With encouragement from Suzie, Gerald launches into his theory of how Scrabble emulates life. He calls it the "Power Web" because it emphasizes the benefit of knowledge, influence, talent, and networking.

"It goes like this, Phil." He sweeps his hands back and forth above the board, like an orchestral conductor. I almost expect the tiles to sing. "To do well in this game, and in life, you first need to acquire knowledge. Not tons of knowledge, just the special knowledge needed to accomplish your task. You can look up the rest. Your special knowledge helps you make the most of what you're dealt.

"Armed with knowledge, you'll be able to maximize the opportunities that come your way in real life. Now, Scrabble doesn't necessarily reward laying down the longest word, or playing a lot of tiles on your turn—even though Suzie and I routinely do so. No, Scrabble is all about wise placement, scoring the most points for whatever tiles you do play. In life, you strive to get the most for the least as well.

"You must learn to pace yourself. Exhaustion is detrimental to success. We came to realize that our score suffered if we concentrated for long periods while playing Scrabble, so we developed the ability to relax when it's not our turn. This clears our heads and when we resume, we see the board and its possibilities much better."

"In other words," the Gnome interjects, "You strive to prevent burnout."

"E-x-a-c-t-l-y!" Suzie replies.

Gerald continues, "Of course, a good Scrabble player tries to prevent an opponent from easily playing off a word laid down. (I think of how I set him up to play "Variedly.")

It's instinctive to lay down your best word, but what good is it if the next player ends up scoring twice what you got? So the moral is, take a chance and plan ahead. What I have just described is the power; this leads to the web."

"It's not the worldwide w-e-b," Suzie offers helpfully.

Gerald smiles contentedly; his grin is large and toothy. "No, it concerns itself with connections. In Scrabble, you need to set up spaces where you can play future words. You build little words so big words can follow. Look at our board. There are irregular lines of tiles branching out in all directions. They are not massed into one quadrant. This provides opportunity for even more branching. In real life, opportunities require a web of friendly people to direct them towards you, and not someone else. So you must build your web."

Suzi offers, "Many people think we just get lucky in life, but there's m-u-c-h you can do to control luck and increase the odds that Lady Luck will, in fact, shine on y-o-u."

They are speaking to the choir; fortunately, I learned the immense benefit of this lesson early in my career.

Suzie has the last word. "Most folks make the mistake of believing Scrabble is a word game. R-e-a-l-l-y, now. This brilliant game is as much about math as it is about words. It is unimportant which words you play because, in the end, only the points you earn matter."

"Is there a lesson in that?" I ask.

"Pay attention to what counts, and not necessarily to what others tell you is important." As she says this, she lays down her final tiles and quips, "Don't be GULLIBLE." *Another bingo.*

My wife will not be pleased to hear the Gnome sand-bagged me. Anna's the much better Scrabble player of our pair and would likely have loved to take my place against the Sweeney buzzsaw.

We conclude our journey into Scrabble land with a drive to a peaceful wooded area where the Gnome points out a sign proclaiming: *Brunot Preserve, Donated 1970 by James Brunot.*

"He became chartable because he could afford to," the Gnome informs me. "You asked earlier, and this is the right time to let you know that Brunot kept most of the royalty money. Still, Alfred made a million dollars up to and including the buy-out by Selchow & Righter and was quite charitable himself."

"So Brunot made a lot more, right?"

"Maybe five times as much. Still, he was the missing link for Alfred, who was on the verge of quitting. If Brunot had not come across Criss-Cross words, if Jack Straus hadn't hung around to play Scrabble in the Hamptons, if an established game company like Selchow wasn't able to help with production, there would likely be no immortal game to honor today."

Alfred Butts lived to be a week shy of his ninety-fourth birthday. Brunot lived to be eighty-two. $G_2 O_1 O_1 D_2 B_3 Y_4 E_1$.

CHAPTER FOUR

THE EMPEROR'S RACE

Nothing prepares me for the sensory assault I experience along this tributary of the Ganges in New Delhi. *Wow.*

It's early morning and I'm already sweating as we walk within a stone's throw of the Yamuna River. I may be lightheaded after flying 7,200 miles and crossing nine and a half time zones (yes, there is an extra half), but my nose is not oblivious to the odor of garbage wafting through the yellow air as lazily as the brown water drifts along the Yamuna.

A few minutes ago, we passed a funeral pyre along its bank. Upstream, I notice women bathing in the water and brushing their teeth. I look back; men have just shoveled the ashes of the wood and cremated bodies into the river, whose ambling current also carries along, in the direction of the ladies, an assortment of debris too defiant to sink.

The Gnome is following a path illuminated on his iPhone. We turn right and find ourselves on a sidewalk crowded with people, flanking market stalls and shanty housing. The teeming mass pours onto the street itself, causing a massive traffic jam. No one seems particularly upset. The aroma of food cooking, spiced by curry, slowly overcomes the aroma of the refuse. But the cacophony of sounds and voices is deafening. Animals appear at random—a goat standing on a low wall, a flock of birds flying just above eye level, then suddenly a street-crossing cow (it crosses unimpeded, as cows are sacred, of course).

One hundred meters ahead is our destination: The Red Fort; the Gnome has told me there's a game inside. One is awed by the enormity of this fortress whose immense walls are made of red sandstone, giving the fort its name. These barriers extend farther than the eye can see. "It's shaped like an octagon," the Gnome informs me. "Inside the Red Fort, an entire city once existed within its two hundred fifty-six acres."

256 acres. As we pay five hundred rupees each to gain admission (about $7.25), I remember my grandfather's farm being about 130 acres in size. My younger self thought that was huge. Once inside, "normalcy" slowly returns; the dissonance fades. The chaotic traffic disappears, as does the swarm of pedestrians. Even the air seems to cleanse itself.

Within minutes, the massive walls are out of sight. We follow a winding path surrounded by parkland, woods, temples, and museums. I am agog. The architecture, even the British-built, is very appealing. I pause to study my map. The Gnome is waving me to catch up. "It is here, Phil. I found it."

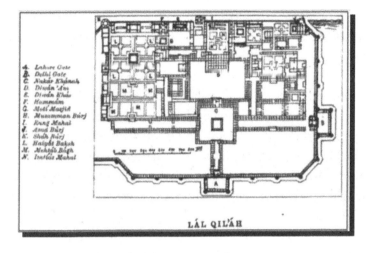

A. *Lahore Gate*
B. *Delhi Gate*
C. *Nakar Khanah*
D. *Diwān 'Am*
E. *Diwān Khas*
F. *Hammām*
G. *Moti Masjid*
H. *Musamman Burj*
I. *Rang Mahal*
J. *Aned Burj*
K. *Shah Burj*
L. *Haiyat Baksh*
M. *Mehtab Bagh*
N. *Imtiaz Mahal*

LÁL QIL'ÁH

In the center of a huge courtyard, he jumps onto a four-legged dais and points to the surrounding pavement where inlaid marble squares form a giant cross-shaped Parcheesi board—or, more properly, a "pachisi" board ("Parcheesi" being the American version's trademarked spelling).

The game path looks much like the one printed on a modern Parcheesi board, only its spaces are narrower, and it lacks the large starting circles. I think about how the game plays. Parcheesi is a race. Each of the four players attempts to move his set of four "pawns" from Start to Home (in the center) before any opponent does likewise. Two dice are used for movement. Pawns can form a blockade—be safe or vulnerable, and if vulnerable, can get "captured" and sent back to Start. Most kids learn to play when they are seven; my aunts taught me. They loved the game and, accordingly, showed me no mercy.

The Gnome is animated and talking a mile a minute. "The Mughal emperor, Shah Jahan, built this place. It took his laborers ten years to construct—walls, turrets, moats, palaces, gates, and all. At its peak, the Mughal Empire included most of modern-day India, Pakistan, and Afghanistan. At about the time Boston was founded, this empire was the world's number one economic power. Bet you did not know that!"

"No wonder the British were attracted to colonize India."

"Sufficiently so that a century later, they considered it more important than holding onto the American Colonies."

I study my map and realize this courtyard fronts the imposing *Diwan-i-Am* (Hall of Audience) where, according to the map's legend, the emperor Shah Jahan and his successors received those who held grievances. Pachisi must have held great and noble significance to become a fixture in his "judicious" courtyard. I try to imagine a giant Monopoly board inlaid before the steps of the Supreme Court.

The Gnome tells me that another Emperor, named Akbar, was the most important person in the history of the game. "He is the main reason we have come here. A very enlightened chap, I am told. Was fair to his people and absolutely adored the game." The Gnome takes a deep breath and slowly turns full circle on the dais. "Okay," he says as he exhales, folds his arms and closes his eyes. "I am ready."

I stand back and watch the Gnome as he goes back in time. Suddenly, he extends his arms, jumps off the dais, and ambles to my side. "He is up there," the Gnome says. "There's not room for the two of us."

"Akbar?"

"It must be Akbar. He is of modest size. Pleasant-looking, carefully trimmed beard, and dressed royally in a pale blue *jama*—a tight-fitting frock—with a flared skirt. He's wearing a soft hat of the same color and material. Must have been the rage of fashion back then."

I try to imagine Akbar while the Gnome is describing the royal audience, sitting under umbrellas in the background. I don't catch it all.

"There are also many pretty young girls standing on spaces of the board—let me count, yes—sixteen in all. Their footwear is embroidered, and they are dressed from head to toe in rather loose clothing, tied at the waist. Their silk is brightly colored: red, blue, yellow, or green. There are four maidens per color."

I envision a life-sized Parcheesi board with human pawns. This is not difficult; I recall the game's TV commercial from my childhood. "Jump, it's fun. Jump, it's easy. Jump—we love to play Parcheesi!" The little kids seen in the commercial were playing on a life-sized board dressed in Indian garb. *Here is where the idea for that commercial came from.*

"What's Akbar doing?"

"He is tossing little shells, ornately decorated. Ah, I think they are snail shells. He studies the five shells and counts how many are mouth-side-up. He directs two of the green-clad damsels to move accordingly."

The game continues as Akbar throws the shells time and again and the Gnome informs me of the movement of the young ladies. He offers a side comment, "I suspect they are maidens from his harem. Each is more beautiful than the next. I doubt any is older than sixteen."

The Gnome's special "rearview mirror" power seems to rub off on me because, at this instance, I vividly imagine the sight of sixteen teenage girls—dressed in Indian garb as seen in Arabian Night movies—with their regal master controlling their every move. I am really getting into this...until the Gnome elbows me.

"That's enough here. The game will go on for a while. Come on, Phil." As we begin to walk, the Gnome says, "I confess I saw something odd when I went back." He looks over his shoulder. "The Hall of Audience was not there. In its stead, I saw a white palace, dripping with ornaments and trimmed in blue. I wonder why."

I shrug. "Where are we headed?" I ask.

"We have to find Saroj Gupta. We are lucky. She is on assignment here for a year before she heads back to Harvard."

"Is she a historian?

"More like an archeologist. Or, as I like to think of her, a game-ologist. She is compiling an exhibit that includes a study of pachisi's past."

Miss Gutpa, a native of Delhi, is conducting research inside one of the many museums that have popped up inside the Red Fort. She's arranged passes for us at its main door. We are escorted through an exhibition hall filled with magnificent Indian ornaments and led to a plain door marked "Private" in several languages. Our escort opens it. In the well-lit chamber, I see a long table set out with artifacts. The woman standing beside the table bespeaks grace and dignity. She is dressed in white; a purple orchid is pinned to her blouse.

The Gnome approaches her, all smiles, and kisses the back of her hand. He introduces me. I approach Miss Gupta; the orchid's aroma is intoxicating. She says, "Hello Mister Phil. My friend tells me you wish to hear of the origin of India's national game and how, by chance, it found its way across Asia to Europe and America."

Her English is crisply spoken. Saroj Gupta's coffee-colored skin is pure and smooth. Her eyes betray great intelligence. Her white garb subdues her rounded figure. She motions with her hands. "This is my workshop while I'm in residence. Would you like some tea?" She points to a cart.

The room is air-conditioned. I have become a bit chilled. We both respond, "yes." With cups and saucers in hand, we follow her to the long table. She begins, "The word *pachisi* is Hindi and means twenty-five, that being the largest move that can be thrown with its dice, which originally were *kaurii* (cowrie) shells. Miss Gupta points to the first exhibit on the table: a set of five decorated shells, perhaps similar to the ones the Gnome just "saw" Akbar tossing. She draws attention to the next exhibit. "Stick dice were sometimes used—a hold-over from earlier times." I gaze at four ivory "sticks" engraved with dots. "But mainly these were used to play the forerunner of pachisi."

She moves on to the next item: a wooden cross-and-circles game board, not too dissimilar. "The forerunner of Pachisi was a fourth century invention named *chaupar*. The board you are looking at dates from the ninth century, but the game did not change in the intervening five hundred years. Its dice were the sticks you just saw. While its play is similar to pachisi, chaupar was primarily a game of insults among elites. It was expected that you would mock your opponents, especially just before one threw the oblong sticks. Cracking one's knuckles or making rude noises was thought to jinx an opponent. Victory was judged by degree of disgrace, according to how many men were left on the board when one player prevailed."

"Sounds like a wonderful way to build friendships," the Gnome offers.

We come to a large pile of cowrie shells. "For centuries, the shells used as dice in pachisi had monetary value. Fifty were worth a few pennies, by modern standards."

We continue to a group of color photographs of game pieces located in other museums, and massive boards inlaid in the courtyards of two other palaces. The Gnome is drawn to one. "The white palace!" he exclaims.

Miss Gutpa looks over her shoulder. "Why, that's Emperor Akbar's palace at *Fatehpur Sikri*. That's his board in the photo. Akbar, more than anyone, salvaged the game and gave it new life."

"Did he ever play here, in the Red Fort?" asks the Gnome.

"Well, no," replies Miss Gutpa. "His palace was built during his reign in the mid-1500s, The Red Fort was completed in 1639 by one of his successors, Shah Jahan. Akbar had died thirty-four years earlier."

"I see…" says the Gnome, mesmerized, mumbling. "I projected his palace, even though I wasn't there. And…" Miss Gutpa asks what he is talking about. The Gnome recovers. "I always believed Akbar held court here."

"Common misconception. Akbar's love of the game made it a fixture at courts built after his time. Shah Jahan carried on the tradition in the Red Fort. He was a fond player of the game, as well. Do you know about the concubines who portrayed the game's pawns?"

"Yes, yes," the Gnome replies. "I saw…" He catches himself and shifts attention to the final item on the table: a long dagger, with a ruby inset on its hilt. "What would this be for?" he asks.

"It would be for you, my curious friend. It represents chaos, personified."

Saroj Gupta tells us a long tale of how chaupar was nearly stomped out by successive wars in ancient India. Pachisi also became little-known and played underneath the surface of India's stratified society—until the rise of the Mughal Empire.

"When Akbar took power, he brought the game back into the open. It began to breathe with life once again because of his imprimatur."

"Rather like a famous celebrity endorsing a product in a TV commercial," I suggest.

She concurs. "Rather, yes, only one hundred times as meaningful." She asks, "Do you know about the magnificence of Emperor Akbar?" We both shake our heads.

"He was far ahead of his time. The Mughal Empire was highly disorganized when he rose to power. There were many ethnic groups and religions within its orders. The traditional way of controlling such a polyglot was through force and regulation. Akbar saw the folly in that. To preserve peace and order, he supported his non-Muslim subjects. He did away with tribal bonds and Islamic state identity. Instead, he encouraged state loyalty by demonstrating *his* loyalty to all his subjects. For example, he abolished the tax on non-Muslims. Soon, the economy was booming, which permitted an expansion of culture. Pachisi was a great symbol of his culture. Play and enjoyment were condoned. He encouraged all faiths. He maintained a powerful military, which deterred envious neighbors from nibbling away at his realm. He presided until he died in October of 1605 from drinking polluted water from the Ganges. Yes, our national problem of bad water is centuries old."

The Gnome seems pleased to hear that his chaos/chance theory is verified once again. "Let me sum up," he says. "Pachisi is vanishing until Akbar comes along. He restores the game. It represents his new philosophy of tolerance and enjoyment as a means to build loyalty to the state, loyalty to him, and to preserve the peace. From chaos and chance, pachisi survives in India and goes on to become its national game."

"Why, yes."

"How did it make its way westward?" I ask Miss Gupta.

"You can thank the British occupation for that beginning in the mid-seventeenth century. Thereafter, pachisi migrated to other parts of their empire, and soon reached England itself." She beckons us. "Come with me."

We approach a large cabinet; she finds a key and unlocks its doors. On its shelves are displayed a collection of pachisi-like games from around the world. My eyes are drawn to a small utensil box, gray and blue in color. Its lettering boldly announces "PARCHEESI." It is sitting on top of an open game board, flanked by dice and cardboard cups. This little package announces: "A Royal Game of India." Its maker is identified as Selchow & Righter—the same company that came to manufacture Scrabble. Miss Gutpa notices my fascination.

"It is reasonable to assume that before the American Revolution, the British brought Pachisi to the colonies. I have studied the game's American lineage. Immediately after the Civil War, a man named John Hamilton, who lived in the Hudson River Valley, copyrighted a game named 'Patcheesi.' He thought this spelling would make it easier for Americans to pronounce as we Indians do. But players mispronounced it as 'pot-chees-y.' 'Pot cheese' is cottage cheese. This association was undignified, so Hamilton changed the spelling to "Parcheesi." At about the same time, E.G. Selchow and John Righter joined together to transform a merchandising firm named Chaffee & Selchow into Selchow & Righter. They were located in Brooklyn and became toy jobbers. Word reached them from the Hudson River Valley; they pursued the lead and made a deal to acquire Mister Hamilton's Parcheesi game."

"It is still with us," the Gnome mentions.

"Parcheesi was your nation's number one game until 1920."

"What worked in India also worked in America."

"It is rather remarkable. Our two cultures are so different. But games are universal. They are built upon basic human needs and desires. Winning a race while in jeopardy and attaining security by reaching home is a universal aspiration. Parcheesi appeared during a time of great advancements in America, including significant inventions like the dental drill, the telephone, moving pictures, and the electric iron. And there were great achievements like the transcontinental railroad, and the first skyscraper. These were accompanied by cultural innovations like the birth of Coca-Cola®, the ballpoint pen, and even the Indianapolis Motor Speedway."

"And a few nasty wars," I add, "Like the Spanish-American, Second Anglo-Boer, and First World Wars."

"Parcheesi endured through them all. And so did its counterpart in England."

She points to another game on display—this one is entitled "Ludo."

"Pachisi was played for a long time In England before this trademark edition appeared in 1896. As you might guess, the name Parcheesi is largely unknown in Great Britain. Everyone there thinks our game was always called Ludo." She pauses, then draws our attention to several more foreign language editions in her cabinet. "As you can see, the game has quite an international following. Each country seems to have its own favored name for our national pastime." I see a copy of *"Mensch ärgere Dich nicht"* from Germany, *"Petits Chevaux"* from France, *"Non t'arrabbiare"* from Italy, and on it goes.

Miss Gupta slides out a lower drawer—the shallow kind typically used to store maps. It contains three more games, and I know every one of them. She explains, "Pachisi is the founding father of a category known as track-pursuit games. You're looking at three of its many decedents, all of which originated in the Western Hemisphere, developed their own following, and can be readily purchased in stores today. There is Sorry!® which originated in England during the early 1930s. After Parker Bothers acquired rights in 1935, it began its best-selling run in the United States. Rather than dice, cards are used to determine movement; its game board track includes special slides and Sorry! spaces. Otherwise, it is pachisi. Next is Aggravation®. Up to six players can play this one and it also has a few twists in the rules. It was initially marketed back in 1960 by the CO-5 Company," she notes.

"I never heard of that firm," I remark.

"That's because it disappeared after Aggravation was purchased by Lakeside Industries, which was a well-known game company for decades."

"Yes, it was."

"The final game is Trouble®, which employs the clever Pop-O-Matic® mechanism to rattle one die under a clear dome. Little kids especially like its simple play. Kohner Brothers launched it in 1965. Winning Moves makes all three of these games now."

Miss Gupta slides closed the drawer and locks the cabinet. "I hope I've been of help, but my work calls. We've just found some items in a badly-damaged wood box dating from the twelfth century. They appear to be pachisi related. I must oversee their rather delicate extraction."

"The game must go on," the Gnome contributes.

"I am glad for your mention of the word 'game,' Mr. Gnome." She looks at me, with a question in her eyes. "Mister Philip, what exactly is a game?"

"She likes to ask this question," the Gnome advises. "She is building a consensus."

"It is important to be precise in life. We've spent all this time taking about Pachisi without discussing which of its features qualify for it to be deemed a game, rather than an activity, a sport, or a mere pastime."

I hear myself reply, "A game is structured by rules, employs special equipment, and has means to keep score or to eliminate a contestant. Perhaps, most importantly, it also includes a clear definition of what constitutes victory—how to win. A game can be small enough to play on a table, or a large sport played outdoors and in arenas."

She nods in agreement, "Fine, very fine. And I would say that if any one of these are requirements is missing, one does not have a game. Correct?"

"I think so. Unfortunately, the term 'game' is used incorrectly, *especially* when one or more of these elements are lacking. I'd like to add one more thing—a true game needs an element of chance, even if such uncertainty is the result of one person's skill versus another's skill. Otherwise, the outcome is the same every time, like the ending of a movie."

She makes a satisfied sound. "I am compiling a list of criteria to judge a game's effectiveness. For example, there must be freedom to play or not to play."

"The gladiators of Ancient Rome had no such freedom," the Gnome interjects. "So one can hardly call theirs a game or sport."

She continues. "The need for equality is another criterion. All players must have the same chance to win, even if handicaps are required. That is why children do not fear playing with adults when they are as equals. Winning a game against a grown person is often a child's first victory in an adult-dominated world."

"I remember how empowered I felt for that very reason," I tell her.

"And I have been told," the Gnome adds, "that the mostly luck-based, watered-down Parcheesi variant *Mensch ärgere Dich nicht*—which means literally, 'Don't annoy yourself'—is played with every child in Germany in order to teach how to accept losing."

"Beneficial. My next criterion is the need for active participation. Today, many leisure activities lead people into passivity. But not a true game. One must be active when playing a game."

I suggest this as well. "Games bring people together from all walks of life and across all generations."

"Shared common experience."

"I will offer one final criterion of a great game," says the Gnome. "I relish a game that makes you dive into it. To leave reality behind. Yes!"

"You seem to do that better than anyone," I remark with a laugh.

On this note, we bid farewell to the erudite Saroj Gupta, with a promise to reunite one day at Harvard.

As the Gnome and I are walking under the arch of the fort's massive Lahori Gate, I realize we have yet to talk of the wisdom imparted by Parcheesi. I remind the Gnome of this omission; he is attempting to hail an undersized taxi. "I haven't forgotten," he shouts over the dim of the throng waiting to get into the fort. "Come on, there is our ride." I cough on the yellow air as I weave through a group of smiling children. They take my photo with their phones. "Bye-bye, American!" they call happily.

We land at Miami International, check into a hotel, and rest all too briefly before the Gnome drives us north on Interstate 95. "Where now?" I ask.

"The world's biggest Parcheesi fan lives up the road in Delray Beach."

"I have an industry friend in Delray," I comment idly, suppressing a yawn.

"He's waiting for you," the Gnome replies.

"Richard?"

"Yes, Richard."

We enter the palm tree-lined drive of the stately yet inviting home belonging to Richard and Sheryl Levy, longtime friends of mine. "You sure Richard is expecting us?" I ask the Gnome. "I think of Richard as a Renaissance Man who happens to like Parcheesi. But is he an expert?"

The Gnome laughs. "Is Richard ever half-way about anything? He can be a serious dude, too."

I rummage through my mind before the Gnome turns off the key. I've known Levy since the early years of my career some forty years ago. He is one of the most positive people in an industry peppered with cynics. He never has a bad word to say about anyone, including scoundrels we both have known, although he has this knack of appraising them with the clearest of vision. I've wondered about the immense store of energy he possesses. Richard has worked for Paramount Pictures, Avco Embassy Pictures (where he launched thirty feature films in foreign markets), and the U.S. Information Agency's Television and Film Service; produced dozens of documentary films; is responsible for the publication of perhaps two hundred games and toys (most notably *Furby*®, which has sold more than seventy million units!); authored books; and has, with his wife Sheryl, visited more than 125 countries and every U.S. state capital. Oh, and he speaks five foreign languages having lived in Spain, France, Italy, and Panama. *Whew!* You can't make this stuff up.

Richard is standing in the doorway, arms open, looking much the same as when we first met years ago. The only difference seems to be his shiny dome is now flanked by gray rather than black. Otherwise, same engaging smile and—most notably—same "patented," oversized tinted glasses. "Phil!" Richard says after embracing the Gnome. "How was India? You know, Sheryl and I went to the Red Fort in Old Delhi a few years ago. At one point in the tour, our guide asked us if we knew what was special about the courtyard where we were standing. I looked around. No one in our tour group even ventured a guess. But, when I saw the stone riser in the center a paroxysm of excitement overtook me. I realized I was standing (drum roll) on an ancient pachisi board. Clearly, this was a gift from the game gods. I mean, this is my favorite game!"

A fine Parcheesi sets awaits us within—not on a game table, but on the carpet in the living room. His dynamic daughter, Bettie—a talent and events producer in the music industry—

greets us. Sheryl comments, "Bettie and Richard have been squaring off over Parcheesi since she was knee high. They like to provoke and cajole each other. Just watch."

"We play an aggressive game," Richard replies. "It's part of the fun."

"I just love this game," he says, as the Gnome and I also join Bettie on the carpet and while Sheryl gets ready to be the referee. "I mean, you've got an immense variety of gameplay choices. To blockade or not to blockade, capture or not capture. When to run, when to lay back. The suspense of rolling at the end to bear off, hoping for precisely the right number. And there's the sound of the dice when they rattle around in the little paper cups. I would know that sound anywhere."

We play. Dice rattle. Cups tip. Cubes roll onto the board. Pawns are moved accordingly; doubles earn a bonus and a free turn. *Yes!* Two pawns on a space form a blockade that no other pawn can pass. Capturing a piece earns a twenty-space bonus move and sends the captured piece back home. A pawn is safe once it enters its home path; getting it "Home" earns a bonus move for another of the player's pawns. However, reaching Home is a bit of a challenge; an exact roll is required. And that's about it for rules.

At one point, Richard reluctantly gives up a blockade and Bettie makes her father pay for it. Richard must have been compelled to make similar moves in prior games because Bettie says, "Once again, catch me if you can!" Her father has, apparently, wasted time maintaining this blockade and watches in angst as one of his now-vulnerable pieces is captured and sent back to start.

I have unusually good luck. I actually think I can win… until the Gnome captures my fourth pawn just before it reaches the safety of my home path. Bettie is beaming with confidence; Richard, having recovered from his restart, just needs a "four" to get his final pawn home. He doesn't get the chance. In dramatic fashion, Bettie rolls a double, earns a bonus roll, and throws a 1-2. She wins before his dice can rattle.

"I often think of Aldous Huxley when I play Parcheesi," Richard says. "He describes games as islands in the vague untidy hands of experience. Parcheesi is my favorite island."

Bettie adds, "You must not be paying attention while vacationing on your island, because I just won."

"Indeed." Richard shrugs. "So here's the bottom line; here's what Parcheesi has taught me. I know there's luck in every throw. I can't control that. On the other hand, I can't control what life throws at me either. I have to decide how to deal with every roll it tosses my way. I have to reason. Now, to some, that's pure work. But it's work that pays off if you keep a cool head."

"I know you're a fan of risk management, Richard," I note. "Does Parcheesi have anything to do with this appreciation?"

"Absolutely. With every move, I identify strengths, weaknesses, opportunities, and threats. This game helps me hone my skill level when I evaluate risk and opportunity in real life. The great thing about a game is you can sharpen this skill without risking any chips. While you can gamble in real life if you want, if you have this urge you inevitably pay the appropriate toll."

The Gnome adds, "Even the dice are instructive. Do you split a roll by moving two pawns, or combine them to move just one? Can you meekly hide on a safe space, or is it better to put more distance between yourself and a threat? Parcheesi requires you to think through meaningful options."

"Parcheesi is not for the timid," Richard says. "Every time I get set back, I resolve to make even bolder moves to catch up. I'm successful in real life because I strive to make good decisions, plan well, and prioritize."

While Richard is a great communicator to the masses, I know he is also a gifted teacher in a learning environment. I ask him to give us one closing "pearl," as if he were behind the podium in a college classroom. He is up for the challenge.

"This game entails examination of structures of thought implicit in all cognitive reasoning problems, assumptions, concepts, empirical grounding, implications, and consequences."

"I see," the Gnome says, though I'm not sure how much he—or any of the rest of us, for that matter—understood.

"What I mean is: Parcheesi delivers the full monty of real-world situations. Always has and always will. No computer can teach you this. That's why the game has earned its immortality."

CHAPTER FIVE

THE DOCTOR AND THE DOUBLE NOT

*I*t's a beautiful fall day to be in Boston. The leaves are just starting to turn color above Copley Square. People are strolling through this small park, taking in some sun, relaxing by the fountain, or—like me—absorbing the famous buildings surrounding it: Old South Church, Trinity Church, the venerable Boston Public Library, and the glassy John Hancock Tower.

Two elderly men are playing chess on a stone table's surface. The Gnome leads me to a spot nearby. "This is where the game Halma began," he says. "Most people don't know that it became Chinese Checkers."

I start to say something, but the Gnome's eyes are glued to the table. A playful dog distracts me as he zones in. "I see the doctor who created Halma. He is seated at a similar table and explaining to a friend of his how it plays. He sets out its game board. It is square and made of cardboard. The playing field is a grid."

"Chinese Checkers is played on a six-pointed star-shaped board," I remind him. "Usually made out of tin."

"That came later," he says firmly. "Do not distract me. I see little pawns being taken out of a bag and set along adjoining corners."

"Who is this doctor? What is his name?"

"George Howard Monks. He's a slender man, nicely dressed, with a boyish face aside from a large black mustache. He is about to start his career as a surgeon here in his native city.

"He graduated Harvard medical school in 1880, four years ago, and was sent to Europe to intern for four years. He's telling the man sitting opposite how grateful he is to be home, having found his four years in Europe to be disjointing, hectic, and higgledy-piggledy. He explains that to keep his sanity, he devised a game of skill in England—having come across a children's game called Hoppity, which involved jumping pawns over each other. Halma is a Greek word, he says, and means… his friend answers 'jump' before Monk does."

"Who's his partner?"

"Thomas Hill. He is much older, and I see a cane propped against the side of his chair. He is stocky, longish hair, thick beard. I understand he was rather famous in his day; a man dealt a full hand of cards—as they said back then. He was a mathematician and a scientist, as well as a clergyman. Great educator, too. He served as president of Harvard University until his health began to fail. He is retired now, in his mid-sixties. Young George Monks holds him in awe. He's hanging on Hill's every word."

"What's the game look like, again?"

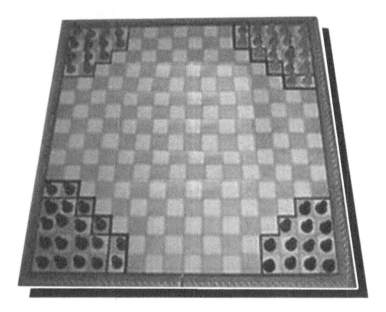

"Curiously, it is a fifteen-by-fifteen grid, same as the Scrabble board Albert Butts settled on. In each corner, a group of spaces is outlined. Monks and Hill seem to be debating the size of these corner areas. In his corner, Monk has set down nineteen colored pawns—they are quite small—and is encouraging Hill to do likewise. They begin to play. They're moving their pieces just like in Chinese Checkers. Oh, there is the first jump. Unlike other games, jumped pieces in Halma are not removed; they serve as stepping stones."

The Gnome narrates the entire game. I grow tired and take a seat. The two players then debate their experience. "Looks like Hill has convinced Monks the board's grid should be sixteen spaces on a side. He seems accepting of nineteen pawns when two people play, but advises fewer when three or four play. Monks is making notes with a pencil on a small pad. He agrees and tells Hill that thirteen pawns would likely be best.

Neither gentleman appears to be contemplating a six-player version, there being only four corners on a square gameboard.

"That is it," the Gnome says. "They are closing up shop. Let us go find an ice cream parlor."

I contemplate Halma as I spoon my butter pecan treat. According to the Gnome, it was the game that became Chinese Checkers, but he has not mentioned how it evolved. I ask him why. "I don't want to spoil what our next expert has to say," he replies nonchalantly. "Besides, good ice cream is to be contemplated and savored."

We drive north to Salem (perhaps derived from "Jerusalem"). Founded in 1626, this "City of Witches" was the longtime home of Parker Brothers. Parker is gone now (its buildings replaced by a housing development). Hasbro, headquartered some sixty miles away in Rhode Island, owns its legendary games. And as for witches, Salem continues to capitalize on its "Halloween" connection to the seventeenth century witch trials, even though they were actually held in the adjoining town of Danvers (which split way from Salem). (Danvers is the home of Winning Moves games.)

Among Salem's most distinguished edifices is the Peabody Essex Museum (the "PEM"). Its glass atrium roof is shaped like the upside-down keel of a sailing ship. Salem was the most important seaport on the East Coast until Mother Nature filled in the bottom of its harbor. Its sailors and whalers journeyed as far as China. As we walk towards the museum's stylish main entrance, the Gnome informs me we'll be asking for Lucy Allbrite. "She's doing research there, and prefers to be called Meg, Margaret being her middle name."

Once again, passes await us, including tickets to the "Chinese House" where she will be found. This building is outside the museum. According to the guide booklet, the Yin Yu Tang House is an authentic eighteenth century home from Anhui Provence in China. It was disassembled, brick by brick, and rebuilt in the museum's rear courtyard. It is imposing—almost as big as the courtyard itself. Its outer walls are fortress-like and devoid of windows. The two-story house is built around its own inner courtyard. The rooms facing the courtyard have large windows. "There is no other Chinese house like this in the States," the Gnome observes.

Lucy "Meg" Allbrite is working on the restoration of a pump handle in one of the homes' two kitchens. She is fair and studious. Her skin shines without any trace of makeup. She might not concur, but I think she bears a resemblance to Jennifer Aniston. We introduce ourselves. "Call me Meg. Well, geez, Phil, isn't it something that my friend, the Games Gnome, has brought you here to a piece of China transferred to America in order to talk with me about Chinese Checkers?"

After briefing a co-worker, Meg leads us along Derby Street. She's taking us to her home to see her collection of Chinese Checkers games. Along the way she comments, "Of course, the game is neither Chinese nor does it play like Checkers. Its name, therefore, it is a double not." We share a laugh.

Meg's clapboard house is fronted by a picket fence interlaced by vines of wisteria. Above her front door hangs a hexagonal symbol. I realize it is a miniature Chinese Checkers board carved out of scrimshaw. She takes note. "The wailers often had long return voyages; they wiled their time carving whalebones. I found this in a yard sale down the street. It was made during one of the last voyages during the 1920s."

Dozens of Chinese Checkers games are neatly displayed among the rooms in the interior of Meg's eighteenth century home. "You're quite a collector," I observe as we enter her living room.

"Well, geez, it started off by accident. My grandmother gave me her tin set and I rather liked its design. Then I saw another in the museum's collection. I became curious and familiarized myself with the game's history. Next, I found six games in a box at a flea market. And now, all this!"

"I've heard similar stories of passion from several members of the AGPI," I tell her.

"AGPI? What's that?"

"The Association for Games and Puzzles International. It's a nonprofit. I'm serving as its current president. Its members are quite enthused, like our Parcheesi expert, Richard Levy."

The Gnome speaks. "I was responsible for its founding, some thirty-six years ago.

The AGPI advocates research into the history of games and puzzles and encourages their collection and preservation.

"Go to games and puzzles dot org," The Gnome advises. "It is your cup of tea."

Meg makes a note and provides the answer to a question stuck in my head ever since the gnome and I left Copley Square.

"Phil, although Halma was invented by an American, it gained its first fans in Europe. In 1892, the German company Ravensburger introduced this version." She points to a cardboard, star-shaped gameboard. "They called it *Stern-Halma*, which means 'star-jump.' It's smaller though—just ten pieces per player.

"Nearly three decades went by before a design patent was granted to a man named Stadnick from St. Louis Missouri for a star-shaped gameboard. His game was only for three players; each tries to advance twenty-six pieces to the opposite unoccupied star point. There is no specific name for the game on his patent, by the way. Oh, and the patent holder may have been a bootlegger."

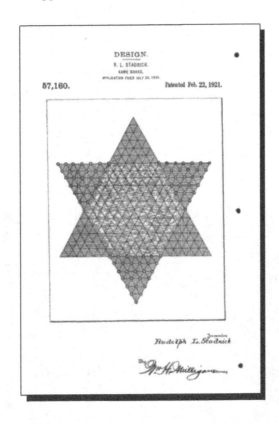

"Ah, the Roaring Twenties!" The Gnome is suddenly agitated, as if a bee has crept under his cap. "Prohibition caused *such* disorder. The Woman's Christian Temperance Union had noble intent, but talk about an ill-conceived law—that Eighteenth Amendment. How could a congressman in his right mind think a law prohibiting the sale of alcohol would persuade people to stop drinking? It had vast unintended consequences. It made drinking more glamorous, more daring. We got bootleggers and speakeasies, bad liquor, and gangsters. The government never authorized enough agents to enforce the law, so when the amendment is shot down during FDR's first term, is it not something that a new game emerges from that chaos?"

Meg absorbs and goes on. "That man's original six-sided game didn't amount to much, but it endured long enough for Bill Pressman and a salesman from J. Pressman and Company to stumble across it in the Midwest. Jack Pressman and Bill decided to call it Hop Ching Checkers Game." Meg points to her copy.

The Gnome lights up. "Ah, I see! A wood frame around a punched gameboard. Did you know the punching technique dates back all the way back to games made in 1892? It was adopted to torture cardboard soon thereafter."

The holes in Meg's Hop Ching board accommodate small balls, not pawns. It may well mark the origin of the use of marbles as playing pieces.

One of the great merits of Chinese Checkers is simplicity. You only move one marble on a turn and no marble is ever removed from the board. You aren't trying to conquer, you're simply trying to rearrange, so it's a novel race game. You aim to be first to move all ten of your marbles across the board into the opposite triangle.

Players take turns moving a single marble of their own color. A marble may be moved into an adjacent hole or it may make one or more jumps ("hops"). Each hop must be over an adjacent marble and into the vacant hole directly beyond it.

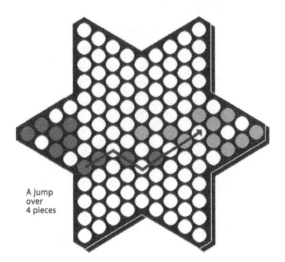

A jump over 4 pieces

Any marble may be hopped and in any of six directions. After a hop, the player may stop, or continue to hop over another marble. A player might even be able to hop a marble from the starting triangle across the entire board and into the opposite triangle in just one turn. That's quite a thrill.

You can move a marble into any hole on the board including holes in triangles belonging to players on either side (but must move out of such a triangle during the same turn). Once a marble has reached the opposite triangle, it may not be moved out of that triangle, only within it.

The first player to occupy all ten destination holes is the winner.

Meg shows us a Chinese Checkers game made of tin. I realize that this is the version of the game most people would say is "the real thing." She hands it to the Gnome.

"It looks like an old friend," he exclaims.

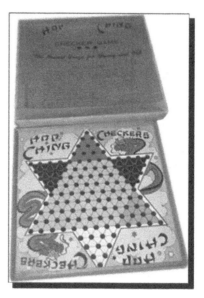

Meg tells us, "Back in 1922, toymaker J. Pressman Company was founded in New York City. Six years later, it likely struck a deal with the originator. Jack Pressman—the firm was named for him—eventually decided that its name should simply be 'Chinese Checkers.' In the Roaring Twenties, all things Chinese were in vogue. The great tile game Mah-Jongg had swept the nation earlier in the decade. People dressed in Chinese garb, lit Chinese lanterns, and ate Chinese food—a passion which hasn't faded."

"Jack Pressman jumped on the rising Chinese star," I offer.

"His timing was perfect," says Meg. "And unlike Halma, Chinese Checkers did not fade away in the States. It became a big seller and still shines brightly. The only hiccup was the Second World War, when metal rationing put the kibosh on tin gameboard production. Jack Pressman temporarily resorted to torturing cardboard, as you guys say, die-cut to accommodate the marbles. Jack built an entire business around this game. Eventually, his firm became known as Pressman Toy Corporation. It endured for decades, run by his widow, Lynn, after his death, and then by son, James. Recently, it got sold to a Dutch company."

The Gnome looks around and says, "But your collection has Chinese Checkers games from many makers!"

"Well, geez, the game was difficult to protect legally. Dozens of manufacturers jumped on the bandwagon after the war. Demand was strong. Every family, it seemed, wanted to own a set. Supply kept pace."

Meg points to her prized possession—a Chinese Checkers game dazzling to behold and kept under glass. "This game was made, we believe, for Prince Rainier the Third of Monaco when he was ten years of age. Its board is not made of tin; it is real silver. The marbles are not aggies, they're made of precious metals and stones, such as rubies, emeralds, gold, and onyx."

The Gnome's eyes are shining. "My distant cousins in Geneva would vibrate if they were looking at this treasure right now. Are you sure these pieces are the real deal?"

"Geez, they look real to me. I want to leave it at that."

"How did you come by it?" I ask. Meg demurs. "That's a story for another day."

The toy industry's Hall of Fame is on display in the impressive Strong Museum of Play in Rochester, New York. There are backlit illustrations of key "players" in the hundred-plus-year-old American toy business, one of them being Jack Pressman.

Photo by Phil Orbanes taken in the Strong Museum

"Meg, do you think Jack's game has any instructive value, any lessons to apply to real life?"

We take seats in her cozy kitchen. She offers us coffee. "I believe it does. First, Chinese Checkers teaches the virtue of not walking alone. 'Work together' is its underlying theme. You need to jump over the opposing pieces as you go, then consolidate your marbles together at the end."

"That implies," the Gnome says, "that it is best not to leave anyone behind, or any task undone. If you strand one of your pieces in its starting position, it becomes extremely difficult to win the game."

"So true," Meg replies. "Wait up for the ones who are lagging and help them advance. As far back as ancient Greece this adage was known and accepted: 'united we stand, divided we fall.' Chinese Checkers exemplifies this advice."

"Inspiring."

"I can think of one more," she says. "Use your opponent's strengths, his position, to help you advance. In life, this suggests offering something of special value to gain what you urgently need."

To cap off this pleasant afternoon, Meg hands each of us a Chinese fortune cookie. "This tradition is also not of Chinese origin. It started in San Francisco in 1918."

"And apparently, the originator was Japanese," the Gnome informs as we crack ours open. "What fun."

Mine reads: "Look past a person's name to his soul. That's where his real name resides."

CHAPTER SIX

A MAN OF MANY SEASONS

W e're standing on the corner of 92nd and Lexington Avenue in New York City, gazing at the neighborhood grocery across the street. It's evening and the river of rush hour pedestrians has dwindled to a stream. Below my feet, the brakes of a rumbling Lexington Avenue train screech. A dozen or so disgorged passengers rise out of the ground. When the train sets itself in motion, a breeze swirls through the sidewalk grating, rustling my pant legs. Rather pleasant, given the late summer heat.

And now I wait, impatiently, for him to go into his trance and tell me why we're loitering here, looking at bananas and potatoes.

He transforms quickly. "Wow, she's just come out of the adjoining theater with that nerdy guy by her side." The Gnome's voice is enthralled. "I wish you could see her, Phil. No wonder she ruled her times."

"Who?"

"Marilyn, of course. The cameras are rolling. According to the theater marquee, she and Tom Ewell have just watched *Creature from the Black Lagoon*. Marilyn seems bothered by the heat; she diverts and stands over a subway grate. Oh my, a gust of air from a train has caught her white skirt. It's billowing up past her knees. The director says cut and asks her to do it again…and then again. The crowd approves. There must be a thousand gawkers around me! Zowie!"

Zowie. The Gnome is channeling Joe E. Brown from Marilyn's 1959 movie, *Some Like It Hot.* "When is all this happening?"

"September fifteenth, 1954. Like I said, wish you could be here with me."

"Calm down, Gnomie," I admonish. "Did you divert here just so you could see Marilyn Monroe film her most famous scene?"

The Gnome makes a disapproving sound; I am obviously too dense to appreciate his brilliance. "Two big cultural events happened on this day, Phil. This one here in Manhattan while only thirty miles away James Brown is finishing the creation of his game, Careers®."

"James Brown, the soul singer?" (I'm jesting.)

"No, Doctor James Cooke Brown, soon to become a professor at the University of Florida. But at this moment in 1954, he is working as a statistical analyst for a large research firm. We will pay him a visit after two other must-see places in Manhattan."

The Gnome leads me into a neighborhood bookstore. It's a combination of old fixtures and new lighting. "I'm gazing at the best sellers on this day in 1954," he informs me. "I see *The Power of Positive Thinking* by Norman Vincent Peale—a book that is still selling. Oh, and there's the topical one I'm looking for: *Why Johnny Can't Read*. It advocates teaching phonics in school systems, a new idea at the time. And it sounds an even bigger alarm."

"And that, Phil, is why we are in a bookstore. In the glow of the postwar boom, worries have cropped up that American kids are falling behind. Education is not adapting to modern needs. Children learned by rote and are trained for narrow occupational choices, many of which are outdated. Meanwhile, a growing demand for scientists, engineers, and technicians goes under-filled." The Gnome adds, as an aside, "The book sells for two bucks. The newspapers at the register go for a nickel."

"What are the headlines?"

"The Russians are rattling their nuclear sword...and the evening editions say there were massive flight delays up and down the East Coast due to storms. Good thing we weren't flying back then, eh?"

"Right...tell me more about the educational crisis. How does it relate to Careers?"

The Gnome snaps his fingers. "Uncanny timing. When the game appears on the market, career planning and better education are drumbeats in America."

"You say this is in 1954?"

"Yes, definitely."

While I did not see Careers on store shelves until 1957, reminiscing about the game makes me want to play again, and not just for old times' sake.

Careers was amazing. You won not by accumulating the most money—as in Monopoly and other financial games—but by achieving a personal (and confidential) success formula, comprising happiness, fame, *and* money points (one for each thousand dollars you accumulated). You could devise any formula as long as it totaled sixty points, which you recorded under a flap at the top of your score sheet.

You traveled around the perimeter of the game board and carefully decided to take inside paths representing different careers and college. In the 1950s, the game's vicarious thrills seemed as vivid as today's virtual reality. My sixth-grade classmates and I played Careers countless times. It certainly made me think about having an exciting career when I grew up.

Dollar signs, stars, and hearts represented money, fame, and happiness. You rolled two dice when moving around the outer path of the board, but only one when moving along an inner "career" path. You gained the opportunity to enter one of these paths if you landed on its entrance and met its requirement—as in real life, credentials were essential—or paid money to fund your endeavor. Four of the occupations were open to you if you had the appropriate college degree. To earn a degree, you needed complete the College path. You could pick a different degree each time you went to college and "graduated." Tuition was five hundred dollars (not inaccurate by the standards of the day!).

Using "Politics" as an example, you could enter if you had the appropriate degree ("Law") or made a campaign donation of three thousand dollars, or you had prior experience—meaning you'd successfully completed the Politics path earlier in the game.

A wonderful feature of Careers was the ability to choose some of your moves, thanks to its Opportunity Knocks and Experience cards. Spaces on the outer track awarded you an Opportunity Knocks card, which gave you the power to move to a particular entrance space (such as "Opportunity to enter Big Business"). As the game progressed and you earned more of these, you became the master of your fate. Sometimes a card even granted you an "all-expenses-paid" admission. Experience cards were earned upon completing a career and by landing on certain spaces of the inner paths. Each granted you a specific move (one, two, three, or four spaces) in lieu of rolling the roll. These cards were crucial to play when moving through a career with nasty negative spaces. "Experience counts" my mother used to say; this adage was born out in Careers.

Every time you reached the Payday space you were paid your annual salary, which increased as the game progressed— for example, graduating college automatically increased it by two thousand dollars. Your score sheet recorded your salary, degrees earned, occupational experience, and most importantly, the hearts and stars you earned during the course of play.

Of course, there were hazards, clever and appropriate. You might lose half your cash in a hailstorm while going through "Farming." You might be caught in a scandal while in "Politics," in which case you gained ten Fame points but lost all your Happiness. And whenever another player landed on your space, you got "bumped" to the Hospital or Park Bench space. You got off the "Bench" (where you were "unemployed") only if you threw a seven, eleven, or doubles on your turn. Exiting the Hospital was tougher—you had to throw five or less, or pay half your annual salary.

The "Florida Vacation" corner space enabled you to rack up happiness points if the dice allowed you to stay put. (In foreign editions of Career, the name of this vacation spot changed to the likes of Majorca, the South Seas, a Country Mansion, the Riviera, or Bermuda.)

The Gnome shakes me out of my private reverie. "Come on, Phil!" he urges as he leads me into the subway. "We need to get to Macy's before it closes, so I can to go forward to 1957."

Macy's flagship store at Herald Square was once a powerful seller of games, as made evident by its role in Scrabble's initial success. I am not surprised to learn that Careers was launched here in New York City, as sponsored by its maker, Parker Brothers.

The Gnome and I are standing in its lobby; he's zoned out again. "It's October fifteen, 1957, about three years later.

I see a giant Careers board on the lobby floor. People are walking all over it. And there's a big Careers sign, right in your face. Cannot miss it. Stacks of the game are for sale. They go for three dollars. And they are selling briskly. It is not just because of Parker Brothers' big promotion, it is also because of Sputnik."

"The birth of the space age!"

"The Russians launched the world's first artificial satellite only eleven days ago. Everyone, it seems, is already clamoring for us to catch up with the Russians. The recommendations in *Why Johnny Can't Read* are no longer debated; they are as gospel. Doctor Brown's Careers game seems prescient; college and careers are destinations on the highway of the future."

"I see what you mean by uncanny timing."

"Phil, the Parker Brothers salesman is talking to the games buyer of Macy's. I cannot quite make out what they are saying because the crowd is buzzing. Something about how well the Careers campaign went over at the Marshall Field Department Store in Chicago. But this Macy's event is more gangbusters. The salesman seems to be boasting that Careers will outsell Monopoly if its TV commercial creates this kind of frenzy across the States."

"The crowd will arise," I say.

Courtesy of the Strong, Rochester, New York

"Case closed!" the Gnome pronounces. He leads me onto the sidewalk and into a taxi and directs it Grand Central Station. We board a Metro North train; the Gnome informs me we are heading for Croton-on-Hudson, some thirty-five miles way. At 10 p.m. the Gnome and I are met at the Croton station by a gnarled, elderly man whose face remains a mystery to me, shadowed as it is by a broad-brimmed hat. The Gnome asks, "Are you Larkin?" After his confirming nod, we enter the rear of the black sedan. Its engine purrs; we leave behind the lights of the small village and plunge into increasing darkness.

"What's this about?" I ask the Games Gnome.

"Larkin is taking us to a place where he played as a toddler, before it became the Institute, as it was known in these parts. It is where James Cooke Brown's stress, caused by jarring chaos, compelled him to invent Careers. We must experience it by night."

As the Lincoln Town Car labors up a winding lane, I catch its name: Prickly Pear Road. We stop only upon reaching the summit of this small mountain. We jump out. Far below, I see lights twinkling along the Hudson. I'm guessing we're six hundred feet above. But when I turn around, a massive fieldstone rampart confronts me. I'm thinking: This is the castle from *Monty Python and The Holy Grail*. Of course, it is not. In the gloom, I realize it is part of a brooding mansion. Three stories tall, perhaps thirty or more rooms—an imposing Gothic "castle." Larkin leads us to its front door; he unlocks it and quickly negotiates a security system. No lights are turned on; instead, we follow the bright cone of his flashlight up a flight of stairs. Three arch-topped windows along the climb let in the pale light of the moon. We enter a hallway and are led to a small room. Larkin waits in the hallway; we step inside. The Gnome produces his pocket flashlight, but before flicking it on, says, "Phil, close your eyes; the current surroundings will only mislead you."

The Gnome takes a deep breath; I hear him exhale. "I am going back once more to 1954. This edifice was the home of the Institute for Motivational Research, which had great influence over the advertising messages bombarding American consumers." He murmurs, and shakes and then says, "Ah, there he is, facing me behind his desk. Brown. He is a pensive man of moderate height, probably in his early thirties, and he bears a resemblance to Sean Connery, no joke. It seems he is working quite late—not uncommon in this results-driven organization, but he is actually moonlighting. He is engaged in a hushed conversation with a man whose back is towards me. A friend, I suspect. They are discussing a deal. Namely, how Brown will compensate his pal for helping him perfect a new game. The prototype comes out of Brown's desk and is laid on it; the man stands up to review it. He quietly asks, 'Tell me again how you got this idea, Jim,' and Brown tells him."

The Gnome's narration goes like this: Brown, who earned not one but *three* doctorates at the University of Minnesota following World War II, cashes in by accepting this rather lucrative job at the "MR" Institute. Its clients include America's biggest marketers, like Colgate-Palmolive, Chrysler, and Standard Oil. But it doesn't take long before Brown becomes unhappy here. Pressure is unrelenting to analyze data and compile reports to justify recommendations to these lofty clients. And Brown believes some of the data is being fudged; he finds the atmosphere soul crushing. He takes refuge in game playing. He has become adept at chess, backgammon, Monopoly, and many other significant games. And then he has a dream. In the dream, he is wracked by the need to decide a new career path. He sees a game, whose board looks like Monopoly's, except it's also like a bowl of spaghetti, with career paths going every which way. And it offers rewards beyond money. Monopoly is one-dimensional, money only. This dream game is *three*-dimensional. When Brown awakes the next morning, he immediately begins to sketch it.

"I see his prototype, Phil: the board appears to be from a Monopoly set with a sheet of white paper glued to its surface.

Its spaces are neatly drawn and labeled. It looks just like the Careers layout I saw on the floor of Macy's. There are mimeographed score sheets and two decks of cards, hand-typed on index stock. There are wooden playing pieces and play money."

I recall how "five-and-dime" stores offered packs of play money back then.

"His friend is pointing and offering advice about where to end the Moon Expedition's path. Right now, it concludes at the space prior to Payday. But his buddy argues it should be moved to the space immediately after Payday because this career already has the biggest rewards. It would be too much to award a salary payment after completing it. Brown says, 'Okay, let's try it.' He reaches into his desk and extracts a pair of scissors and a piece of white paper. He cuts a small piece and tapes it onto the board, then draws a new ending space for the Moon path. The friend also has a suggestion for the Opportunity Knocks deck. Brown crosses out a few words on one of these cards and pens new ones in their place."

I comment, "So, if I picture the scene correctly, Doctor Brown has, at this moment, a fairly complete prototype of Careers and is asking for suggestions to perfect it."

"That is how I read it. By the way, his friend is charged up. He likes this game and its potential. He asks Brown what he plans to do with it."

"What does Brown say?"

"Brown tells him that after he makes his next career move, he is going to take a chance and publish it himself. He has saved some money, enough to print a few thousand copies, and he will sell them to game stores from the back of his car. The friend says, 'Wow, that's a big risk. Why not submit the game to a big game company?' Brown replies, 'Because they probably wouldn't appreciate what I have here. This is too futuristic; I have to make it a hit first. When one of them learns about its success, I'll get a good deal.' His friend asks, 'What will you call your company?' Brown replies, 'Brown Manufacturing.' His buddy thinks that is too dull; Brown shrugs."

When Brown and friend begin to haggle over the rules, the Gnome decides it is time to go. He snaps out. Larkin takes us down the mountain to an inn where the Gnome has reserved rooms. Larkin drives off; no words are exchanged.

The Gnome suggests we share some decaf before turning in. "Prior to bringing you here, Phil, I learned about Brown from his last wife, Evelyn, and his daughter, Jenny. Doctor Brown was one hell of a guy. A Renaissance Man. Or, as I now muse, a Man for Many Seasons."

Courtesy of Evelyn Anderson

Courtesy of the Strong, Rochester, NY

Born in 1921, Brown was a twenty-three-year-old navigator on a B-17 bomber when it got shot up badly during his twenty-fifth and final mission in World War II. He helped guide the wounded plane close to its base in Scotland before it crashed into the North Sea. He led the rescue of the other nine crewmembers and got them into lifeboats. They made it to shore.

Armed with his doctorates from the University of Minnesota and experience at the Institute for Motivational Research, he changed careers and accepted a position as a professor of sociology at the University of Florida. While there, he successfully sold and promoted Careers. Word of its success reached Parker Brothers the following year. The phone rang. A deal was struck. In 1957, Careers was launched nationwide by the big game firm. A big hit!

But Brown's ingenuity was just beginning to ignite. In 1955, he created a new language—"Loglan"—which stands for "logical language." (It is still in use today.) Brown wrote science fiction novels, in particular *The Troika Incident,* which prophesized a handheld electronic "reader" that could access a free knowledge platform. This 1970 book called for social change by making education available to all. (I wonder what Brown would think about the Internet and social media if he were living today?) Brown also advocated job planning to guarantee everyone work. "Brown went far after leaving the Institute," the Gnome concludes.

The Institute. A deep, troubling memory suddenly begins to stir inside my head—something to do with a man and the Institute for Motivational Research. Like many distant memories, this one is stubbornly buried. I need a connection to trigger it. I am about to voice this to the Gnome, but he yawns and says, "Phil, let's get some sleep. We have an early flight. We're going to some place really nice this time."

Late the following morning, we land in Bermuda (the Vacation corner's namesake on the British version of Careers), the first bit of paradise the Gnome has taken me to. Its verdant main island is 665 miles off the coast of North Carolina. Its climate is sunny, the waters are aqua, and its beaches are pink. Its colorful flowers seem always in bloom. But with only twenty square miles of land, the natives suffer from "island fever." It's not easy being blessed when you can't go to new places without taking a boat or plane. And while Bermuda has become self-governing, it remains beholden to the United Kingdom for defense and international representation.

We taxi to the Fairmont Southampton Hotel on the island's southern shore. This beautiful pink and white edifice reigns from the island's highest point. It was the "Southampton Princess" when I came here in 1980 to judge the World Monopoly Championship and does look like a high-rise designed in a fairy tale. As I walk up to its main entrance, I am reminded of what Yogi Berra once said: "It's *Déjà*-vu all over again."

Did the Gnome bring me back here to relive that great Monopoly event? Or is this hotel somehow connected to Careers? Perhaps this was a locale frequented by Jim Brown?

We gain permission to enter the hotel's amphitheater. It is decked out with sophisticated technology and multimedia components completely lacking when I presided over that Monopoly contest back in 1980.

This room, however, still resonates with memories. I see the stage where the officials' table was located, with my seat at its center. I remember its backdrop: flags from the twenty-eight nations that sent a national champ to compete for the world title (won by Cesare Bernabei, a charming microwave engineer from Italy, on assignment for RCA in New Jersey).

"There is a faraway look in your eyes, Phil," the Gnome says. "But we are not here to talk about Monopoly."

"Then what does Bermuda have to do with Careers?"

"Think back. It was here where you met one of my best friends. A man I valued so highly, I regarded him as an honorary gnome. A man who, during your stay, talked a great deal about the Careers game."

"Victor Watson!" I exclaim. I begin to recall our inspired conversations.

"Correct. Not only was Victor tournament director, he was the man who came up with the very idea of World Monopoly Championships. You two found much in common when you conversed between rounds of play."

"We become fast friends. We were of one mind, separated only by a generation." Victor was a savvy businessman and a spirited bon vivant. He grew up playing games as I did. I remember his devilish grin and gleaming eyes, one of which tended to narrow as he smiled—as if to suggest he had something up his sleeve, or perhaps because he believed there was mirth to be had no matter how serious the topic. I can see why the Gnome accorded him "honorary" status.

"I'm going to let *you* go back this time, Phil." The Gnome leads me to the outdoor swimming pool. Far below, at the base of the hill, is a lovely pink beach and beyond, the crystal-clear ocean. "Think back to when you and Victor sat out here in April of 1980. You're over there under an umbrella, right?"

"Correct. He began by giving me a peek into John Waddington, the Leeds England printing and game-making firm his grandfather and father had guided for fifty years. Victor's turn to steer came during the 1970s. I gave him the short version of my career, making a joke at one point of how the game Careers helped me realize I was meant for the games business. Turns out the game was pivotal for Victor as well."

"Talk about Victor."

I half close my eyes in order to focus and do just that.

In 1936, Victor was seven when his father, Norman, licensed Monopoly after Robert Barton of Parker Brothers sent Waddingtons a copy. Victor played it with his father several times during the weekend after the sample arrived. And he was at "ground zero" when his father developed the UK version and licensed it throughout Western Europe. His father journeyed to London to decide on locations appropriately valued for property names on the English version of the game. His father went on to discover other hit games like Subbuteo, Buccaneer, and Cluedo. But Victor took the lead in advocating the Parker Brothers game Careers—his first significant contribution while working his way up at Waddingtons.

I tell the Gnome what Victor told me. "So just like Dad got hold of Monopoly from Robert Barton, I took charge of Careers once Barton sent it off and it came through the transom. I loved the layout of the game board, what with it looking like Monopoly around the outside, plus eight paths of travel on the inside. These paths filled the area left unused on the Monopoly board. Brilliant. I told my father we should get this one. His staff gathered, we played, and voted thumbs up. My father asked me to ring up Robert Barton. During our brief call, he told me a professor in Florida had come up with the game and that very little had needed to be changed after Parker took it on. I told Barton that professor must have good game blood in him, because most amateurs tend to throw a spanner in the works when they develop their initial idea into a game.

"I asked Victor if Waddingtons changed the game at all. He replied, 'only to make it ring true to us Brits. To wit, I suggested Bermuda for the vacation corner. Ironic isn't it? Here we are, in this little paradise. Anyway, our timing was perfect, what with Sputnik and science, science, science in the dailies. We were ringing up big sales the moment we announced Careers.'"

"It is actually rare for a game company executive to love games like Victor did," the Gnome offers. "He was special. Zowie!"

Zowie again. I imagine Victor meeting Marilyn Monroe, and this triggers a vivid recollection of what actually happened next during poolside meeting in Bermuda. I tell the Gnome the story.

An attractive waitress appeared and Victor beckoned her. She was blonde and spoke with a lovely British accent. Victor mustered his charm—a natural gift. "Darling, my American friend and I would be delighted to sample something potent and British. I am prepared to trust your judgment." She smiled at him; he flashed his patented grin. She laughed; we watched her disappear into the pub.

I told Victor that what excited me most about Careers as a kid were its choices. While Monopoly dictated your choices according to where you landed, in Careers, choices came under your control by earning Experience and Opportunity cards.

"Wisdom is a lifelong pursuit, best begun when young," Victor offered.

I asked him if Careers provided any pearls of wisdom.

Victor put on his professor's cap and introduced me to… Carl Jung. "Do you know the man?" he asked. "Sort of," I replied. "Well, he's worth the effort. Tremendous insight and all. Jung said: 'Where wisdom reigns, there is no conflict between thinking and feeling.' That's really important, because most of us can't reason when emotion catches fire. That's when we stub our toes." He added, "I learned that the inventor of the Careers game exercised great wisdom while his job was tearing him apart. Do you know the name of the man he was working for at the time? Ernest Dichter was the bloke who figured out that image and persuasion could be manipulated via advertising. Dichter devised depth analysis and focus groups to dig into consumers' desires. Eventually, his reach extended into Europe. We used him."

I remembered Dichter and his nickname: "the Miner." Or more fully, the "Miner of Minds."

Dichter learned how to engineer emotions and inner needs through clever messaging.

"The original marketing devil, to some," Victor replied offhandedly.

I told Victor that General Mills employed his services. His long shadow still hovered over Parker as a result. I wasn't crazy about his methods. When I was younger, working for a small firm named Gamut of Games, I hired his rival—Louis Cheskin—to help with our packaging.

"How were they different?" Victor asked.

I explained that Dichter's focus groups were assemblies of consumers, mainly housewives. They'd be asked to discuss, in depth, what they liked and didn't like about design or copy alternatives. A consensus would be reached. Cheskin, on the other hand, thought focus groups were a waste of time, because the testers were plopped into a social setting and instinctively acted more sophisticated than they really were. Their avowed preferences were, therefore, unreliable. Cheskin used indirect methods, meaning consumers weren't aware they were being tested.

"Well, James Brown of Careers got disenchanted with Dichter and left, right? But Dichter would reign supreme for many years. Eventually he became discredited. Enough of him! I must tell you about a new idea in marketing that's really good. It has piqued my curiosity."

I asked Victor what it was called.

"Prospect Theory. And it pertains to Careers, Phil. Prospect Theory is about economics and psychology. It reveals how people really make choices when faced with options. At university, we were taught that most people choose rationally. *Wrong.* For example, Prospect Theory holds that people opt for certainty over risk, even when the risk is low and the potential payoff with some risk is much greater."

I asked for an example.

"Let's say I have the opportunity to win a thousand quid, no worries. And I have a chance to earn even more, say two thousand, but the odds of doing so are maybe eighty with a twenty chance of losing money. Prospect Theory says that, based on research, most people play it safe and take the grand."

I was intrigued.

"The second part of the theory holds that most people are loss-sensitive. One tends to remember losses much longer than gains, because losses sting and their pain embeds deeper. I won that thousand quid, right? But say I turned around and lost eight hundred of it. I'm still up two hundred, but it doesn't feel good. I focus on the eight hundred I lost, not the two hundred I'm ahead."

Our appealing waitress delivered our drinks—for me, a Tom Collins and for Victor, a gin and tonic. He sipped. "Bombay gin, if I am not mistaken!"

"That's right, sir," she replied, glowing.

"Goodness. You have an amazing gift: ESP!" Victor said playfully. "You conjured up my favorite." I also applauded her selection of my Tom Collins. (I was partial to them at the time.)

"ESP? Not really," she quipped. "Missus Watson and the gentleman's wife are inside the pub drinking Rum Swizzlers. I consulted them."

She quickly departed, responding to a waving hand on the far side of the pool. Victor picked up where he left off. "Next point. People, even we two brilliant minds, are more aware of relative well-being than actual level of comfort; we are inclined to think of how we are doing compared to the next guy It feels much better when one gets a bonus, or a raise—or some sort of gain—if our rival *does not* If I get a hundred-quid bump in pay and my neighbor also gets a hundred, I don't feel better, even though I'm up. Alas, I remain at par with the cad."

I told Victor it sounded like you'd only feel better if that so-called rival didn't get a raise.

"Perversely, yes. So curious how us humans tick. Our clocks are wound by emotion. It's important to know this if you've ever to tame your wild beast."

Hmm.

"Phil, there's a final conclusion to be drawn from this theory's findings. Namely, we all discount the unimaginable, the unlikely. Like losing everything in a disaster, or your job, or your wealth. As a result, many people live on the edge, because this tendency to discount precludes them from proper planning."

I told Victor I knew, from research studies, that most people didn't have more than a month or two's worth of expenses tucked away.

"There you go."

I then asked him how Prospect Theory related to Careers.

"First, most players are reluctant to take on the high-risk careers, like Expedition to the Moon, until they have some Experience cards to diminish the chance bad luck will bite them. But if you wait too long, your opponents will scoop you."

I asked how loss sensitivity related.

"This goes hand-in-hand with avoiding risk. When you follow the path of a high potential career, you tend to remember every space that penalizes you or dumps you on the Park

Bench. You don't appreciate the points you've gained before these setbacks. This pain disrupts future planning. You brain tells you not to try this career again."

I queried about relative positioning.

"Easy. In Careers, I am often reminded of your current salary, because each of us collects it upon reaching Payday. If I increase my salary to ten or fifteen thousand, it feels good until I notice you are at eighteen grand. Then I'm envious and tend to lose track of just how far I've come…oh, there's one more point." Victor sipped his drink before continuing.

"There's that chance you can lose it all. Same is true in Careers. If you get reckless and play poorly, you'll end up on the Park Bench and have a tough time getting back in the game."

I commented, "Careers does dramatize the need for forward planning."

"Indeed. Somehow, a quarter century before it was announced, the inventor of Careers sensed all the lessons of Prospect Theory. Most impressive." Victor raised his glass; we toasted James Brown.

Our waitress returned to see if we'd like a refill. But the next round of championship play was imminent. We bid her adieu; Victor tipped her handsomely.

"That was very kind of you," I remember saying.

"Well, I felt sorry for the poor gal," Victor replied with his Cheshire grin.

I had to play along. "Oh?"

"Phil, you must have heard about the penchant we Brits have for poor planning and unexpected rationing since the Second War." I told him that I knew Cluedo's introduction was long delayed due to a cardboard shortage. Victor nodded gravely. "How true. More recently, I suspect we suffered silk rationing because the lass's blouse was a bit short on material…and they seem to have run short on buttons as well."

And with that I concluded my reverie and returned to the present.

The Gnome quips, "Ah, that is so Victor. Always a clever devil." He asks, "I don't imagine you two talked about any more wisdom imparted by Careers?"

"We didn't have to. His application of Prospect Theory pretty well summed up what you can take away from the game. I, on the other hand, think there is one more lesson to be had. It is this: You gain useful insights into what your opponents value most in life when their success formulas are revealed at game's end. You may learn if they value happiness over money—or fame—or vice versa. Very useful to know."

The Gnome adds, "That Jim Brown was some remarkable guy. Whatever he touched, it seems he sensed its future before anyone else."

In regard to James Cooke Brown, the visionary creator of Careers, his daughter, Jenny, also informed me that she helped her father developed a "Senior" version of his game, which had three more categories of achievement (virtue, power, and enlightenment) and several more career paths. A mainframe computer was used to test its possible success formulae to assure the outcomes were balanced, no matter what the success formula chosen.

*Brown and daughter, Jenny, in 1978,
courtesy of Jenny Brown*

Brown and wife, Evelyn, courtesy of Evelyn Anderson

His wife, Evelyn, informed me that, in his sixties, her husband designed a custom three-hulled sailboat, a trimaran. They sailed it around the world. In 2000, at age seventy-eight, Jim and "Evy" were sailing off the southern coast of South America when Jim's pacemaker malfunctioned. They were rescued by a cruise ship, but not in time. Jim passed on before they reached the nearest hospital, in Ushuaia. James Cooke Brown is buried there, in this former prison town, so very far from home: Ushuaia is the southernmost city in the Americas.

Courtesy of Evelyn Anderson

Ushuaia's radial prison, now a museum, is seen above

Careers went into publication in dozens of other countries. It endured on the US market for decades. During this time, many of its Career paths were updated. After Parker's rights expired, Pressman published it, then Winning Moves Games. Careers would establish an entire category of aspirational games—games of choice—many of which went on to become best-sellers, especially via the medium of computer gaming. Knowing James Brown's uncanny knack for envisioning the future, chances are—if he was alive today—he'd say, "Told you so!"

CHAPTER SEVEN

PARIS AND BRUSSELS, HOT AND COLD

*T*he Gnome is humming Cole Porter's "I Love Paris" from *Can-Can* as we approach number 72 on the *Rue de Belleville* in the neighborhood of the same name. "Ah, there she is," he exclaims with certain pleasure, pointing to a plaque commemorating the little songbird, Édith Piaf, who grew up here and might even have been born under a nearby lamp post.

We're on our way to an art theater to see a special showing of the legendary 1956 short comedy-drama entitled *The Red Balloon* by French filmmaker Albert Lamorisse. "He filmed it around here," the Gnome says, gesturing with both arms extended. "In this very neighborhood." He adds, "Lamorisse also created the game that became known as Risk."

I think: *A movie producer who has the knack to invent a game? I wonder what linked the two within his creative palette?*

Lamorisse's little movie begins; I quickly realize it is a children's story—at least on the surface. I admit to being captivated. *Le Ballon Rouge* features a young boy, played by his six-year-old son, Pascal, who encounters a very bright red helium-filled balloon. This is no ordinary balloon. While it is mute, it otherwise seems alive. It has a mind of its own and begins to follow the boy wherever he goes, even though the boy's mother will not allow it inside their small apartment. Lamorisse's young daughter is seen at one point, with an equally sentient bright blue balloon. The two balloons are attracted to each other. Eventually, Pascal's red companion draws envy from other boys. There comes a moment of tragedy near the climax, followed by an ending that is almost spiritual. The movie turns you into a kid again. (I won't ruin it for you.)

Before the theater lights return, a well-known French movie critic appears on screen to offer a short review of praise. *The Red Balloon* was universally acclaimed; Lamorisse won an award for the Best Original Screenplay in 1956 at the Cannes Film Festival, plus an Academy Award. *The Red Balloon* eventually became a staple of films shown to elementary school children.

When we emerge into the light of day, I realize this neighborhood has changed a lot since Lamorisse's filming. In the movie, the depressing gloom and "gray" of the street scenes provide vivid contrast to the cheery brilliance of the balloon's red color. Perhaps the balloon symbolizes hope and enlightenment.

The Gnome shares his opinion, "Belleville was a dreary place after World War II and fell into further decline during the sixties. The government tore down a lot of the buildings you just saw on screen and replaced them with the brighter, if

monotonous, housing we gaze upon." The Parisians who populated the streets in the movie have been replaced by modern
brethren, who come mostly from Africa and China. There is
also a noticeable increase in the number of *Police Nationale*
patrols (the successor to Inspector Clouseau's *Sûreté*, in the
Pink Panther movies), watching over the neighborhood.

Lamorisse's children's movie and his military game Risk®
seem far apart in the realm of entertainment and age appeal.
Based on the movie, you would think he would have invented
a children's game similar to Candy Land®, Chutes & Ladders®,
and Uncle Wiggily®, which—in addition to their simple messages of good versus bad—are delightful romps. Risk, however,
is heavy-duty and for a much older crowd. The Gnome has
reminded me that, in Carl Jung's estimation, "All the works of
[a] man have their origin in creative fantasy. What right have
we then to depreciate imagination?" It is not my intent to
doubt or demean, but to *learn*.

Risk is a game of global conquest. It awakens a powerful
urge in most adults: the need to own, to control, to be the
master of one's fate. A map depicting the surface of the earth,
divided into six continents and sub-divided into forty-two
territories, is depicted on its board. The aim of the Risk is to
gain control of all forty-two territories by the skillful employ-
ment of dozens of armies represented by little wooden blocks.
When a player wishes to attack an opponent occupying an
adjoining territory (say, from the one named "Ukraine" to
adjoining "Scandinavia"), each player rolls dice. The attacker
may qualify to roll three dice, the defender no more than two.
The higher number(s) rolled prevails, causing the elimination
of an opposing army or two. The defender wins a tie. The
attacker, upon wiping out the defender's last army, slides a

bunch of armies into the conquered territory, and, most bene-
ficially, wins a card. Printed on the card is a silhouette of a foot
soldier, or a cavalryman, or a cannon (artillery). Collect a set
of three identical cards, or one of each, and you may exchange
them for additional army pieces. The value of these exchanges
constantly increases.

Risk is a game for the shrewd and the bold, not shrinking
violets or the faint-hearted.

All this begs the question: why did a boyish-looking thirty-two-year-old, married and with three tiny children, create
such a game while on vacation (which, in 1954, must have
been in August when all of France, it seems, goes on holiday)?

The answer hits me like a brick. I sensed it during the
movie. The 1950s was a decade of unreality in France, itself
a time of chaos. Paris was affected by the unrelenting tension

and gloom caused by the Cold War. Although World War II ended eleven years earlier, the Russians continued to maintain an insanely large military force along the north-south border of divided Germany. It was well within the realm of possibility that they might decide to go from "cold" to "hot" war at any time. Their armies would punch through the thinner ranks of the Western allied armies and reach Paris in a week's time. Every French man and lady over the age of eighteen contended with this apprehension, reinforced by the painful memory of Hitler's forces overrunning France in two weeks during May of 1940. I think of "loss sensitivity" in Prospect Theory.

"Come on," the Gnome commands. "We're going to see where the game took shape."

We taxi to the business part of town and enter an office whose proprietor, albeit uneasily, allows us access to a meeting room. The Gnome has negotiated permission for our intrusion. He tells me this was once the home of Miro, the French game company that published Lamorisse's game back in 1956. I know of Miro as a "sister company" because General Mills owned the firm during my days at Parker Brothers. Michel Habourdin, a big Frenchman with heavy jowls and expressive, rounded lips, managed it. He wore thick glasses and was both affable and cunning. He knew his business and was quite a gamesman. The Gnome says, "Naturally, when Albert Lamorisse sought a publisher for his game, he connected with Miro. This firm, as you know, had relationships with both Parker Brothers and John Waddington. It published the French editions of Monopoly, Scrabble, Cluedo, and other well-known games. Albert came to this very office in 1955. By the way, his game was not called Risk then. He named it *La Conquête du Monde*—The Conquest of the World. Albert set his game in the Napoleonic Era, to avoid the distaste for World War II, and the Cold War."

Nothing in my surrounding suggests the game company Michel Habourdin once ran from this spot. The Gnome is not affected by the here and now. He "zones" and begins to motion. "I am not present on the day Lamorisse first arrived. It is a month or so later. I am observing a critical moment in the game's development. It seems that Albert's original game was rather crude and too big. He had navies on the oceans as well as armies on the land. The game took a long time to play. Much too long to be commercial."

"Who do you see in the room?"

"This is a company-only meeting. Lamorisse is not present, nor is his design partner Michael Levin. I see your old associate Michel Habourdin and he is quite animated. He's talking with Jean-René Vernes, an independent game designer and part-time philosopher. You can look him up. Anyway, Habourdin, affected by the Lamorisse mystique, has agreed to evaluate the game, despite his doubts about the viability of its theme and its imperfect game play. He's given Vernes an assignment: try and make it play well and play quicker. Vernes is back today with his recommendations. Jean Boisseau appears; he and Habourdin own Miro. They listen as Vernes explains his changes. The navies? They are gone; they slow up the game too much. The dice, well, they are still rolled to determine the outcome of battles, but now ties favor the defender. There are now cards, accumulated as the game goes on, which can be exchanged for four more armies each. Habourdin is nodding his head. He is satisfied. Miro will go forward. Six months later, *La Conquête du Monde* is on the market."

Courtesy of David Stewart–Patterson

Photos by Phil Orbanes of game in the Strong Museum

Habourdin had confidence in the appeal of the revised *La Conquête du Monde.* He submitted it to Parker Brothers for consideration in the US market. At this point in their "triumvirate," Miro was the "third" partner. The big sellers in Habourdin's line had come mainly via Waddingtons. Now, Habourdin saw a chance to play tit-for-tat and up his standing, perhaps at the expense of Waddingtons. So be it.

The owners of Parker Brothers liked the game, sort of. As with Clue, they fretted about the implication of "bloodshed" inherit in the game's theme and worried about a name. World conquest equaled warfare and smacked of the horrors of the last world war. Then somebody suggested subtitling it "Parker Brothers Continental Game." *That will work,* the firm's owners agreed. But calling the game "The Conquest of the World" would not do. Not only did it undermine the new subtitle, it did not suggest this was a "family game." Parker Brothers was the leading maker of games to be played by the entire family, ages eight and up. It had shied away from adult-level or male-specific games.

More and more of the firm's management were called in to play the game, and offer opinions about game play, and perhaps suggest a new name. One day, Elwood "Al" Reeves, a member of the firm's sales force—nicknamed the "seven dwarfs" because there were seven of them and the orders they garnered were often considered "undersized"—came in with a slip of paper on which he had written "R-I-S-K." *Wow,* exclaimed the owners. This is really good, how did you come up with it? Al explained that RISK was the initials of his four grandchildren!

Great. The game had a title and a theme but was still plagued by a slow pace. It seemed resistant to improvement.

So the newly-christened "Risk" game languished and was not published in 1958, to the dismay of Michel Habourdin. He began to grumble that he'd like the US rights back from Parker so that he could, perhaps, induce Milton Bradley (Parker's chief rival) into publishing his "baby." Of course, this was pure bravado, because to threaten Parker Brothers would be to lose Monopoly; Miro could not afford that "risk." However, Habourdin's displeasure led to renewed commitment at Parker to "fix" the game.

Robert Barton, the president and recipient of his father-in-law's majority stock ownership, enlisted the aid of up-and-coming Eddie Parker (grandson of the oldest of the original Parker brother). The youthful Eddie approached the problem without the handicap of preconceived "rules" ossified over decades of experience. A World War II naval veteran, he had witnessed the massive delivery of US supplies and men in the last two years of the conflict and realized that the weight of this force had won the war for the Allies—not necessarily tactics or strategy or technology. In a masterstroke, he suggested that, each time a player earned reinforcements (by turning in a set of three cards), it be worth more new armies than before. Pretty soon, so many army pieces would be at the disposal of a player, he could launch an all-or-nothing "steamroller" attack and (hopefully) sweep the board in one dramatic turn—or die trying. The finale of a Risk game became an exhilarating rollercoaster ride. The game play was now as good as any Parker game, maybe even better.

New Parker Bros. Game, "Risk" Requires Skill, Luck, Strategy

"We've introduced some pretty unusual games during our 75 years of game publishing," commented Robert B. M. Barton, president of Parker Brothers, Inc., Salem, Mass., recently, "but Risk, our new continental game, is so different, so broad in scope and sweeping in its moves, we feel it will bring new excitement to the game-playing public of this country. It is, without doubt, the most unusual game to appear in years."

Players, Mr. Barton said, will find Risk thoroughly absorbing because of its originality and daring. It is termed a challenging game, intricate but not difficult; a game that calls into play a little of everything—skill, luck and strategy. And the whole world is the "playing field" in Risk, which embraces continents and spans oceans.

The attractive playing board and the 450 attractively finished playing pieces in convenient plastic boxes (one for each player) are handsomely set up in a colorful embossed box. Risk will bear a retail price of $7.50.

Risk originated in France, where it was known as Conquete du Monde. It was invented by Mr. A. Lamorisse, well-known film writer and producer, and author of the prize winning film, "The Red Balloon."

Courtesy of the Strong, Rochester, New York

Risk finally appeared on the American market in 1959 for the (then) astounding retail price of $7.50 (Monopoly sold then for three $3.50). Parker ran advertisements in upscale magazines that read: "If you have $7.50 to spend on a game, Risk is for you." Price, however, became a non-issue because men and boys (especially preteen boys) *had* to have this game. Its conquer-the-world theme was overwhelmingly appealing to them. (I was one of them.) Michel Habourdin rose a notch in the triumvirate.

Victor Watson was slighted. He once told me, "Michel was envious of the rapport of equals that I shared with Bob Barton. He circled my back and submitted his conquest game to Parker directly. He was quite smug when Parker made it a hit. Only then did he ask if Waddingtons would like it…pegs on a pole and all. Michel was a friend, but also a fox. One had to watch the hen house door."

We depart the building; the Gnome sums up. "Cold War chaos and the chance involvement of other contributors molded Lamorisse's game into a global winner—even in Germany where its military theme was *verboten*. An Italian gaming friend of mine, Roberto Convenevole, wrote a book entitled *La storia di Risiko e l'anello mancante*. In it, he explains how the game's idea in Germany was recast as 'liberating' the world. And, as in Italy and elsewhere, the game was named *Risiko* in Germany." Risk/*Risiko* eventually did conquer the world.

We're not done. The Gnome whisks me off to *Gare du Nord* train station in order to catch a maroon Thalys express to Brussels. He tells me, "I don't really know the guy we are going to see, but he comes highly recommended. He is billed as a Risk heavyweight. Really knows the game inside and out. Has a lot of clout…or is that 'weight'?"

I am curious.

Nowadays, it seems that board game tournaments, organized by enthusiasts, pop up all the time. You might play Scrabble for prize money in New Orleans, Monopoly inside a classroom in San Diego, or solve Clue within a haunted mansion. When we arrive at our destination on *Rue de l'Etuve*, a

Risk tournament is already underway. Today's prize is a bottle of Napoleon Brandy. The winner of this year's round of tournaments gets his name etched on a plaque affixed to a trophy resembling Napoleon's bicorn hat. I study the names of seven prior winners. There's room for three more before a second plaque must be added.

After the next few hours have passed, I conclude that, for a really intense Risk experience, you have to play with "General" Bernard Perpose in Brussels, Belgium—the city that houses the headquarters of NATO. Within the world of Risk, "General Perpose" is known by many names. He's nicknamed "Jeep" for short; we'll get to the others.

While not a real general, Jeep was an officer (rank undisclosed) in the strategic planning office at NATO Headquarters—which is how he landed in Brussels. After finishing his military stint, he ran an internal "think tank" at General Mills European headquarters in Amsterdam. "I've always worked for Generals," he boasts. His many acolytes refer to him as "the General" in good fun.

At NATO by day, Perpose structured mock war games; by night, he and his friends played Risk because, as General Perpose says, "the NATO games were all hypothetical, based on what we'd do if the Russians attacked here, or struck there. Just game theory, not real games. Frustrating." But playing Risk, apparently, proved to be the perfect anecdote. "We'd get together after hours and slug it out over the map of the world. One of us would conquer it. I won my share. We'd eat and drink and feel like warriors, not prissy armchair generals."

The tradition endures. Perpose has left General Mills for a posh job working with a research organization in Brussels. All hush-hush, but it seems that NATO is one of its clients. "Best of both worlds," Perpose says. "Get to help the military without having to follow insane orders." He adds contently, "And now I have plenty of time to play Risk."

Like today, he and his merry band have gathered in the second floor function room of a restaurant with a slightly obstructed view of the *Manneken Pis*—"the Lil' Piddler"— Brussels' most famous landmark. This diminutive bronze statue takes a leak into a fountain basin 24/7, and has since the year 1619. (Actually, the original is in a museum, but its replacement carries on without fail.)

Jeep's followers have rather important jobs in government and finance. So when they gather to play Risk, they inevitably exchange ideas, which contributes to the lure of accepting an invite from the General, who is also nicknamed "General *Porpoise*" because he is a "big fellow" and likes to eat. His salt-and-pepper hair is cut into a thick brush; he otherwise bears a resemblance to actor John Goodman.

At noon, most folks in Brussels choose to dine on *stoemp* or *waterzooi* in one of the medieval city's delightful restaurants. But if you come to play Risk with General "Porpoise," you'll be helping yourself to *pomme frites*, pickles, Swedish meatballs, beefy sandwiches, hardboiled eggs, and lots of breads—all set out in quantity atop a long table conveniently positioned on the flank of the round table (command post) where Bernard Perpose presides while seated in his chair, overseeing the battles being fought on the four game tables in the center of the room. While the General is observing, he tends to reach over to the long table and gobble something, anything, without looking at it. The bread rolls go quickly.

Occasionally, one of the other players takes a moment to come to the spread and load his plate with a few more *frites* and eggs; Perpose nods his approval. But woe to the player who abstains. "Robert!" Perpose will suddenly bark. "You're not eating. Get that man a plate." The waiter on duty—apparently "battle-hardened" by prior experience—hastily loads up a paper plate and rushes it over to needful Robert ("Roe-bear" in this part of the world). Robert handles currency transactions at a Big Bank, so you can bet General Perpose (from now on, I will refer to Bernard Perpose/Jeep/The General/ General Porpoise as simply "Perpose"), urges Robert to talk about current exchange rates for the benefit of the gathering.

Satisfied with Robert's information, Perpose stands and points to a distinguished-looking player peering at the board through wire rims. "Claude, you're not drinking. Dehydration is bad. Get Claude a *Chimay*." The waiter pops a cap off a bottle of ice-cold beer and sets it next to the aforementioned Claude—a money manager at a large mutual fund. Perpose asks about the prognosis for the stock market.

Claude replies, without taking his eyes off the board, "It will fluctuate."

"Don't give me that crap answer by Henry Poor. Give us your gut." (Henry Poor was a founder of Standard, and Poor vacuously uttered these words in reply to a similar question back in 1922.)

Claude clears his throat. "Just like my opponent here," he replies, "It's going down." Claude answered in song, imitating Paul McCartney singing pity lyrics from the Beatles' tune "I'm Down."

This triggers a Perpose smile, "Want to know which musician was a truly great Risk player? Jimi Hendrix. Honest truth. Why? He was a military guy, a paratrooper. I played him; I lost, despite the fact he was really high on something. Remember Graham

Nash of Crosby, Stills, and Nash? Another Risk player. He once said about Hendrix, 'No one ever beat him at Risk.' Truth."

Perpose marches round the room. "Beatrix, my darling, how are things in Immigration? Any new problems?" Beatrix, a studious woman with a matronly appearance, shakes her head "no." Perpose frowns. "You're not eating enough. Get Bea some more Swedish meatballs!" The waiter responds as if electrically prodded.

Perpose continues to "tour the battlefields," and when he sees something noteworthy, he says what he thinks. "Luc, you got the wind in your sails. Europe is yours, but you better watch your back door. Johan is ready to jump you from Africa." Johan demurs; he has struck an alliance with Luc. Perpose sneers. "I give you five minutes before you break it."

Risk is known as a game of forged alliances, associations, and backstabbing.

At another table, a lady with shrewd eyes and a peekaboo hairstyle has just conquered the Australian continent. "My, my, Yvette, you are so clever today. You have the strongest defensive position in any game. But how can you break out? Thierry has armies up the derriere in Siam!"

"You can say 'ass,'" Yvette retorts.

The Gnome builds up the courage to remind Perpose why we're here: to learn his take on the wisdom imparted by Risk.

"Right, Sir!" We take seats at his "command post" while he grabs a plate and builds upon it a pyramid of meatballs, deviled eggs, and frites. "You ready?" We prepare to take notes while he eats and talks rapid fire—fortunately one activity at a time.

"First, be like Luc and make friends with the players whose armies border yours. Keep these alliances as long as it makes sense. Risk is the best game to learn how to negotiate, better even than Monopoly. You have to be good with the tongue to persuade the wolves from attacking you—just like in real life, when it makes sense to keep peace with those who could do you the most harm. Like maybe your boss, your teammates, your neighbors, your wife, if you got one. Don't let your own bloody ego intoxicate you."

Perpose now gives us four more tips. The first two are common with other games we have studied. Keep a reserve for a rainy day; don't spend all your resources in an orgy of expansion—plan and spend prudently. Next, learn from failure; have a back-up plan for when things go wrong. ("They do all too often, right?" he quips.)

His final two gems are new. "Watch your opponent's eyes. They will narrow when he or she begins to plan to cause harm. In other words, learn to read people and don't ignore the suspicion invading your brain as they begin to shift from friends to adversaries. Finally, don't become insular, like Yvette. It is great to have a safe place, but the world does not reward you if you withdraw from contact with others or fail to conquer your fears."

"Perfect. Thanks so much," the Gnome says. "Five invaluable tips."

"Make that six," he snaps. "I saved the best for last. Don't get caught playing a game of chicken." Perpose summons another beer for each of us.

"You see my two friends over there?" He points to a pudgy bureaucrat named Michel and a wiry diamond merchant named Ollie. "They keep threatening to attack each other and try to show they mean business by piling armies into their adjoining territories. They got blinders on. They are becoming increasingly vulnerable to attack elsewhere, by the other warmongers at the table. If they don't call a truce, they'll both end up on the dust heap of history."

"Chicken?" the Gnome asks.

"Everybody plays Chicken at some time or another. We used to 'war game' Chicken at NATO." Something else occurs to him. "Do you guys remember the movie *Rebel Without a Cause*? Chicken got its name from that movie, when James Dean and that other guy drove their cars towards a cliff like maniacs to see which one would jump out first."

I recall the movie, and I know something about the underlying idea of this game Chicken. "You're talking game theory, right? Von Neumann and all." I was into game theory while in college.

"That's right, hotshot. Game theory is an analytical discipline that deals with irrational behavior. You can apply it when playing Risk. At NATO, we had to game every possibility between us and the Warsaw Pact countries."

"Enlighten me," the Gnome requests.

"Okay. I'll involve you and Phil in a simple example. Get up and follow me." He opens the door to the hall and positions the Gnome on the outside, looking in, and me on the inside, looking at the Gnome. "You each want to go through this narrow door, right? But you're nice guys. How do you decide who goes first?"

"We motion the other to go first with a sweep of an arm," I demonstrate.

"Fair enough," says Perpose. "But what if you both are equally polite? Who will enter?"

The Gnome rubs his beard, "We stand by for a second or two, then one steps out of the way."

"All right," says Perpose. "But the one who stands down loses, right? Think of it as a game. You win if you go through first. The other guy loses."

I comment, "But not fully, because he gets points for being more polite, if that means anything."

"Isn't this just trivial?" says the Gnome. "How does this apply to Risk?"

"Go sit down, both of you." We oblige him. "Michel and Ollie are so wrapped up in pounding their chests, they don't see how vulnerable they've become. Risk reminds me that Chicken can be deadly serious. Kennedy and Khrushchev were playing apocalyptic Chicken back in 1962; their game involved nuclear missiles. Kennedy did not swerve. Khrushchev flinched. The White House relied on game theory to decide every escalation to convince Khrushchev the 'crazy' Americans would use the nuclear option if he persisted."

The Gnome voices another example. "Hitler played Chicken with Chamberlain several times. And he won consistently because Chamberlain was not about to go to war."

"Right," says Perpose. "Then Churchill comes into power and the next time Hitler tries Chicken, Churchill convinces the British government to say 'F-You' and Hitler eventually gets stopped, then defeated."

I think of something else. "For a long time, the nuclear arms race itself was a game of Chicken, wouldn't you say? We'd build more missiles, then the Russians would do the same, or vice versa. The more missiles with nuclear warheads lying around, the more the risk of one being launched."

"This was our biggest worry at NATO. All those weapons, piling up on top of each other. What if someone on the other side did decide to launch a tactical nuclear weapon somewhere in Germany? How should we respond? That was part of my job. That's why, to this day, I hate to play Chicken."

The Gnome has the final word. "Taking Chicken to heart in real life, you need to know when it is time to cut your losses, otherwise things get out of hand. Better to take a small loss than to lose a bundle."

"That's right, little guy." Perpose lifts his bulk into a standing position. "Now, I got a tournament to run. I play in the final game against the four table winners. I think Luc's on his game today. I gotta watch him again."

Perpose leads us to the stairway. "Chicken is only one kind of game we played based on game theory. There were many others. Fascinating tool. Tortures your brain, though, unlike Risk." He eyes the waiter, who snaps to attention. "I'm thirsty. Bring me something good, will you?" We part at the door. The Gnome goes first. Perpose snaps. "Chicken! You lose Phil."

As we walk back to the Metro, I ask the Gnome. "Did Albert Lamorisse ever invent another game?"

The Gnome shakes his head. "No, he did follow the progress of Risk as it spread around the world. He approved a few variations of his game as time went by. He enjoyed his royalties; they paid for more documentaries. But he didn't live long enough to really appreciate his game's success."

"What happened to him?"

"Lamorisse died in a helicopter crash in Iran back in 1970 while shooting his latest documentary. He was only forty-nine."

Chapter Eight

THE BRILLIANT JERK AND THE DOWNTOWN SAINT

Reykjavik. I think: Too bad proper nouns are not permitted in Scrabble. R-e-y-k-j-a-v-i-k could earn one heck of a point haul. The capital city of Iceland is new to me, but not the Gnome. It lies only two degrees south of the Arctic Circle, which means it gets very little sunlight around the winter solstice. Given all that darkness, its highly civilized residents (120,000 plus strong) are firm believers in elves and gnomes (ours is in his glory).

However, the Games Gnome is not your diminutive garden-variety gnome, so he only draws a few looks of curiosity as we head for the Laugardashöllin arena, the scene of the chess "Match of the Century." He casually mentions that his maternal "line" blended with paternal humans a long time ago. Perhaps the second look he garners is due only to his red cap and pleasant beard.

Nonetheless, a country that reveres gnomes is a "great one" in his opinion. Iceland is technologically advanced; it survived a national bankruptcy during the Financial Crisis of 2008–2011. Yet Icelanders are perpetually worried about offending the "little beings" and take great care to avoid getting on their "bad side." For instance, sudden bends in a road are due to avoiding locales where these creatures are thought to dwell. Seriously.

US chess champ Bobby Fischer didn't care a wit about this predilection when he arrived here in early July of '72. He was preoccupied with the belief the Russian KGB were out to get him.

That Bobby Fischer arrived here at all is a story unto itself, which unfolded for me as a close bystander. I keep this to myself for now. The Gnome has gained access to the big room inside the Laugardashöllin where the championship began.

"What do you see?" I ask as he enters his zone.

"Nothing, unfortunately. We have to move to where most of the games were staged. Follow me."

We enter a much smaller room—it's like a large closet (there is a chess set on a table; apparently a local tournament is scheduled). So why was the main room was abandoned in 1972?

The Gnome reconnects with the past. "It is Game Three. Fischer is down two games to none—to reigning world champion thirty-five-year-old Boris Spassky—because of a questionable move he made in the first game, plus an outright forfeit of the second game. Seems Fischer had made demands and decided not to show up after the officials declined his ultimatum."

"Did Fischer relent?"

"No. Spassky decided it would be undignified to win the championship via default, so he yielded. Fischer had insisted the championship move to this small room, without spectators. Spassky, who was quite confident, obliged him."

From what I knew of the then-twenty-nine-year-old Bobby Fischer, his seemingly childish behavior was par for the course. "What's happening in Game Three?"

"Fischer has shockingly moved his knight to h-five. If you did not know his resume, you would think he was a rank amateur—the move is that weird." The Gnome quickly reprises the game for me: Spassky, moving the white pieces, tried to rattle Fischer with a little-used opening. However, Fischer, playing black, was unfazed and countered with the predictable defense until moving his knight to the side of the board. You can almost hear Spassky thinking: *What the F-?*

"How does Spassky respond?" I ask with bated breath.

"He takes Fischer's knight with his bishop. I mean, after all, that knight is dangling. Fischer, in turn, takes the bishop but his overall position now looks weaker than Spassky's." But as the Gnome describes the next several moves, it becomes clear to me that Fischer had a hunch he could lure Spassky into chasing him like a dog following the scent of red meat. In so doing, Fischer's position grows stronger and stronger and Spassky's becomes disorganized, and he can't regain the initiative. In chess, the initiative is often so valuable that maintaining it is worth being down a piece or two.

Several moves later, the Gnome animates, "Wow. Spassky is rubbing his forehead. He just risked moving his king towards the center. Fischer took the Russian's second knight and now Spassky's king is exposed and in check. Spassky seems punch-drunk…my God, he resigns!"

Bobby Fischer would go on to win twenty-one out of the twenty-eight games played.

The entire world followed these games that summer. It was the Cold War in microcosm. Soviet supremacy versus American aspiration. The rigorous Soviet system versus American adaptability. Spassky kept expecting Fischer to open with an orthodox King's Pawn opening; Fischer would not oblige. Spassky was ill-prepared for the alternatives thrown at him across the chessboard. Both players made obvious mistakes, but Spassky made far more than Fischer.

By the time the tournament concluded on August 31st, a crowd of global proportion was storming retail stores to buy chess sets. The contagion spread as fast as a virus. Chess Fever gripped the world. Millions upon millions of chess sets were sold, some with fine wooden boards and pieces, but most with boards made of tortured cardboard and pieces molded from plastic.

The magnitude of chess's sudden popularity was astounding given the erudite nature of the game, its difficulty to learn (let alone master), and its foreign pedigree. Its earliest forerunner originated in sixth century India and migrated to Persia a century later, where it was refined but languished until the eleventh century when it captivated Europeans. Five hundred more years passed before the queen became the most powerful piece on the board (real queens would dominate that era) and the game we know today was "finalized."

The Gnome leads me back into the main room. He zeros in and informs me he is "there" on August 31, 1972. Pandemonium reigns. Reporters are clamoring for interviews, dignitaries are popping champagne and..."Victor Watson is here!" the Gnome exclaims.

Victor, of course! After witnessing this frenzy for chess, he envisioned a World Monopoly Championship right here, which he masterfully organized and held in this venue during the fall of 1972. Talk about striking while the iron is hot.

"I wish I could have been there," I confess to the Gnome. "I would have loved to revel in Victor's dry wit and hear his off-hand remarks about the Match of the Century...and to drink ourselves silly, of course."

After a night in Reykjavik, it is my turn to surprise the Gnome. "We're not flying back to Boston," I announce. "I made a switch. We're going to JFK and I'm taking you to a location in Lower Manhattan that has everything to do with chaos, chess, and Bobby Fischer."

"You know something I am not aware of?"

When we reach John Street, I point to a modest office on the second floor. "In 1972, that office was part of Davis & Davis, a father-son legal team. I was working my first post-college job in York City. Two years earlier, I needed some urgent legal help. My new friends in the games business introduced me to the son, Andrew P. Davis. Andy not only helped me immediately—problem solved—but he only charged me a token fee. I came to learn that he had a weakness for talent in need of legal protection. My friends referred to him as 'Saint Andrew.' But it wasn't until the summer of 1972 that I learned 'Saint Andrew' was also Bobby Fischer's lawyer, and that Andy had never billed Fischer a dollar for his services, despite prodigious hours."

The Gnome absorbs this. "I must assume that somehow Saint Andrew, as you call him, had something to do with the 1972 world championship?"

"If not for Andy, there would have not been a tournament."

"How so?"

"Imagine it is June twenty-nine, 1972. Hemlines have dropped. *Grease* is just beginning its run on Broadway. Uptown, the first Star Trek convention is taking place. Volkswagens putter along every thoroughfare in this neighborhood. You could take a family of four to that restaurant across the street and dine for five or six dollars, tops."

"Fischer," the Gnome reminds me, suggesting I stay on topic.

I get to the point: for five straight nights, he was supposed to board a plane bound for Reykjavik. On five consecutive nights, he failed to show up. In three days' time, Bobby had to take his seat across the chessboard from Spassky, who was already there, rested, and waiting. That night was the last night Fischer could fly before the Sabbath and arrive in time to get a good night's sleep. It *had* to be that night.

Earlier, Fischer was awakened from a deep sleep by a clever reporter who tried subterfuge to gain access to his hotel room. After thwarting him, Fischer got scared. His imperative was to pick up the phone and call the one man he knew could help him: Andrew Davis. Davis said, "Okay. Stay calm. I am sending friends." Within the hour, marketer Herb Hochstetter and limo service operator Morris Dubinsky turned up and began to stand watch. I knew them both. It became their job to get Bobby packed and ready to go to the airport.

Their charge was a *wunderkind*, a paranoid genius…and a jerk. They knew that.

From Davis, I later learned that Fischer had grown up with a homeless mother and no father. His mother was schooled in Moscow but came to America after anti-Semitism spiked during Stalin's rule. The FBI investigated her when Bobby was young. Bobby's first exposure to chess was at age six, thanks to a cheap cardboard set purchased at a candy store. His interest in chess was instantaneous. As he grew older, he joined chess clubs and learned at the feet of chess masters. He won the US Junior Chess Championship in 1956. He was a Top Five US player by age sixteen, when he decided to leave school in favor of chess. By 1965, despite also dropping out of the chess world for a while, he was a seven-time US Champion. He also began to believe the Russians had fixed world chess, and that the KGB had tapped his phone. Despite his growing paranoia, by June of 1972, Fischer's chess point ranking was the highest of all time (2785 to champion Spassky's 2660).

So why was Fischer so seemingly reluctant to get on an airliner to Reykjavik? Why was the media examining him under a microscope and branding him "a spoiled brat" or a "jerk" while his rivals were calling him a "monster"? Why was he allegedly terrified of women? Why was he pegged a monomaniac? Clearly, something in his wiring was amiss.

But you wouldn't detect this at first glance. Fischer was tall and vibrant. Handsome, broad-shouldered. On second glance, however, you'd become suspicious. His chess-savvy brain was housed in a smallish cranium and, combined with his low forehead, he evoked a rather primitive impression. A lock of hair liked to dislodge itself and hang over that brow. His eyes, on the other hand, seemed to radiate danger—like a hunting cat's. He was a fast walker but tended to lurch while moving towards his destination. According to Davis, Bobby had difficulty juggling two thoughts at once because he was so accustomed to singular focus on one task—that task usually being his next move on a chessboard.

Bobby Fischer was "different." Quite different.

By contrast, the Andrew Davis I knew gave off no alarming signals. He was a quiet man of forty-three years. Slim and of medium height, he wore professional specs and would break into a big, warm smile at the slightest note of humor. However, when Bobby Fischer was in his charge, no humor was in the offing. Andy confessed that he viewed Bobby as a delicate vase filled with a priceless liquid and destined to be poured on some great occasion or broken into pieces beforehand. Davis had taken a private oath to keep this vase from breaking.

Fischer had stonewalled Davis, and everyone one else who wanted him in Iceland, because he thought too few reporters would fly there to cover the match. He thought the purse much too small, even though money itself seemed like a foreign object to him. Nonetheless, if boxing superstar Muhammad Ali enjoyed a take in the six or seven-figure range, why shouldn't a chess superstar be worthy of similar compensation? And then there was that worry about Russian subterfuge. Spassky was enthused about the venue being Iceland. *What did that suggest?* What had the sinister KGB arranged to help Boris and harm him?

To unravel this knot, Davis took Bobby to the Yale Club for a meeting with two of the tournament's organizers. They offered Bobby a deal. It wasn't quite enough, until a British investment banker, Jim Slater, threw in more money and Davis helped persuade Secretary of State Henry Kissinger to ring up Fischer and give him a pep talk about how good it would be for morale if he, on behalf of America, prevailed over an adversarial Russian. Fischer's icy resistance finally melted.

Hochstetter, Dubinsky—and big, teddy bear-like Bob Hallowell (a game industry entrepreneur who published some of my games)—got Bobby into a Cadillac and drove him to JFK Airport. Once there, Fischer found his cold feet again and attempted to "escape." Davis helped negotiate a two-day delay. Only then did this petulant man-child aim his awkward stride towards an airplane door and make history.

The Gnome lets the pre-story of Bobby Fischer's journey soak in. He smiles. "Once again, chaos and chance lead to good things in the world of games."

"What do you have up your sleeve regarding wisdom?" I ask. His eyes light up. "You have conveniently brought us within blocks of the answer. We need to head uptown to Park Avenue."

In the taxi, I tell the Gnome that most game players I know don't think chess is a good teacher of life's lessons because it is an abstract game of strategy, devoid of luck. I do note one exception. My long-time game inventor friend, Rene Soriano, thinks chess is actually a good model of society because, as Rene puts it, "When things get dicey, the pawns go first."

"Your friend, Rene, makes a valid point," replies the Gnome. "And your other friends are wrong." He then tells me that the man he is taking me to is: "A self-made multi-million-aire whose mastery of chess helped him to rise from poverty and gain a good education. His name is Walter Zupan. 'Wally' if he knows you. Otherwise, Mister Zupan."

Mister "Wally" Zupan lives in one of those venerable high rises on Park Avenue on the Upper East Side. A doorman asks you to wait, ever so politely, while he confirms your intended visit. An elevator operator, outfitted in forest green with gold piping, assures your smooth rise to the seventh floor where you step into a small, elegantly appointed foyer; two doors lead from it. Mister Zupan's is on the left. His manservant (yes, there still are a few) opens the door and ushers you onto marble flooring that reflects the bulbs of overhead chandeliers. I notice over my shoulder a sweeping staircase leading to the upper level of this duplex. A turn of a corner brings us into a sitting room whose walls are lined with Old Masters, worth heaven knows how much. Our destination comes next: a handsome library upon whose dais stands a study table some centuries old. A large chessboard sits upon it with official "Staunton" pieces, made of rosewood and maple. We take seats along the sides of this table and await Mister Z. I imagine him as mysterious and remote, like a mountain hidden behind clouds—or perhaps he is a recluse like a monk in Tibet. Or perhaps—like some other super wealthy individuals—he has morphed into a cruel judgmental man prone to condescension.

Not unexpectedly, I am wrong. After the muffled click of loafers on the staircase, a man appears dressed in casual clothing with hand extended. "Zupan here. Welcome, welcome." I notice first the curls of graying hair on either side of his shiny baldpate. His eyes are large and remarkably deep blue in color. His weathered face is merry, and his mouth smallish. His lips are not cruel; they settle into a contented smile. Here is a man who, it seems, is quite happy with himself.

"I knew Bobby," he informs as our drinks arrive. "We were both born in 1943, he in Chicago and me in Europe." (Zupan is not more specific.) "We both came to America at about the same time and each enjoyed the blessings of poverty, if you will.

"Bobby did not know Hans Gerhardt Fischer, his father—who, by the way, was a brilliant biophysicist of German extraction. My military father died while I was quite young. Our mothers saw to our schooling; mine worked two jobs so that I could begin Yale. I played at most of the same chess clubs as Bobby and employed my growing skill as a means to an end. I made nice money playing the game. Enough, in fact, to spare my poor mother the need to work such long hours. After I graduated, I learned how to invest the money of others. I applied my lessons learned over the chessboard and, I admit modestly, I made wise choices. So I am retired today, but I left my firm, and its billions, in good hands. I now spend about thirty minutes each morning making my picks."

(Which, I assume, means the stocks he elects to buy and sell.) "Otherwise, I play games."

The Gnome informs me that Zupan is not only accomplished at Chess, but bridge, backgammon, the Japanese game of Go, and—indeed—Monopoly.

"You and I think alike when approaching the best way to win at Monopoly," he advises, "but I understand you are not here today to talk about your signature game. You want to know my chess secrets. Do you wish to play opposite me as I opine?"

I think of the Sweeneys and their Scrabble dominance and quickly demur. I do not wish to agonize against his genius, realizing the slightest mistake on my part will spell doom. Besides, I know my limits. My younger son began to regularly beat me in chess when he reached the advanced age of eleven.

"Chess is like a beautiful woman," Zupan begins. "Endlessly complex, eternally mystifying, always changing. To attempt to know either is to take a journey from the known to the unknown. To survive the unknown, one must develop the skills to cope with every possibility." With that, he says, "Call me Wally."

Wally then reveals his knowledge—or some great portion of it; I suspect that, like Colonel Sanders, his "secret sauce" is off limits.

I take notes. His dissertation goes something like this:

1. Chess teaches the need to focus, to think with agility, and to plan ahead. Most importantly to imagine yourself in the other fellow's shoes and figure out how he sees you.

2. Chess also teaches the need to make *well-considered* decisions, because every decision counts on the road

of life. Bad ones toss you into a ditch. Good ones speed up your progress.

3. Every move has a purpose; it should not be made on impulse, despite the urge to avoid hard thinking. Their purpose is to play for an advantage, and once you get it, to maintain it. If you don't seize the initiative, someone else will make a decision for you and you probably won't like how it turns out. *Play the game or the game plays you.*

4. A chess match only clashes two players, but in life, everyone is playing. Some of the other players are your friends but many are not.

5. Don't become predicable like Boris Spassky in 1972. Ignore what your opponent is doing at your own peril. Learn to apply lateral thinking. George Bernard Shaw once said, "Two percent of people think, three percent think they think, and the rest would rather [lose] than think."

6. Get rid of clutter and distractions. In chess, that means exchanging pieces until only a few are left on the board. Doing so can make it easier to secure checkmate. In life, it means recognizing your strengths and focusing on them. Whatever else competes for your time runs interference, like a charging lineman in football.

7. We don't win every day. Minimize your losses and move on.

8. Don't become emotional or take things personally. (Wally acknowledges the difficulty of doing so in everyday life.) Listen to what people say and watch what they do, but don't target the people. In other words, play the board not the player. Win gracefully;

lose gracefully. You need many friends to get ahead in life. (I think of Gerard Sweeney's "power net.")

Eight points, clearly stated. I am glad the Gnome brought me to this man. We relax and chat about nothing of consequence until he shows me a photo announcing the new Bobby Fischer Memorial at the Harpa Concert hall in Reykjavik.

"It is good of the city to honor him," Wally says. "He died there, you know. So odd."

Fischer's contorted mind convinced him to abandon his title, and it wasn't until 1992 that he again agreed to a match in Yugoslavia against Spassky, which he won along with $3,500,000. But by playing, he violated a United States and United Nations Security Council Resolution against Yugoslavia—which he had been warned about—and ended up a fugitive who bounced around Europe until he re-entered Iceland to live, and died of renal failure at the age of 64.

Bobby Fischer, the malcontent, did however draw undying admiration from chess players, especially the masters he played against who considered his brilliance on a level so lofty as to rewrite the principles of expert play. Perhaps more importantly, Fischer connected the masses to chess, which further assured its distinction as mankind's most significant game, worthy of immortality.

"Too bad he could not bask happily in its glow," the Gnome laments.

We bid Wally adieu. "See you soon," the Gnome says as we head for the door, as if he's coming back tomorrow.

CHAPTER NINE

THE PRINCE AND THE SHOWMAN

As we regain the sidewalk, I wonder where among the globe's seven continents and seven seas the Gnome will next take me.

"We are only walking seven blocks," he informs as we head south on Park Avenue. "Before we get there, I am going to tell you a story as good as any fairy tale, involving a fine prince and his favorite game. Here is how I remember the story."

Once upon a time, a Russian boy was born into nobility. He would grow up to be tall and slender, and he would possess compassion, perception, and intelligence. He would make a difference. But when he was just an innocent child of three, evil men toppled his nation's government and decreed death for all those with means who had supported it.

The Evil Ones aroused a crowd of supporters who lost their humanity in the contagion that followed. Their new-found thirst for blood was unquenchable. It was predicted a million would die, but by the time the Bolshevik purge ended with the death of Joseph Stalin in 1953, at least twenty million of Russia's people had been exiled or murdered.

When it began in 1917, chaos quickly reigned throughout the land. There was no hiding from the Evil Ones and their followers. All possessions, except money, had to be abandoned in the flight to survive. Among those who managed to escape Russia were the little prince and his parents. Late that same year, despite the Great European War, he and his parents somehow reached the safety of Paris. The boy's parents missed their home-land and already knew they would likely never see it again.

A few years after the Great War ended, they immigrated to America where their sadness would disappear like clouds following a storm. They felt blessed to be in the United States, protected by its rule of law, which guaranteed their human rights, and afforded its opportunities. When their son—the prince—graduated high school, they sent him to the University of Virginia because Thomas Jefferson had founded it. Jefferson had regarded this achievement as more significant than serving as the nation's third President. Upon reaching manhood, the prince rewarded them by working hard as a real estate broker, dividing his time between New York City and Florida.

Prince Alexis Obolensky made many friends and they affectionately nicknamed him "Oby." He liked his occupation, but his love, his *passion*, was reserved for a game.

Backgammon (and its predecessor games) is of ancient origin, perhaps mankind's oldest. It had surged in appeal during the 1920s and '30s. The prince stumbled upon the game by chance when he noticed two acquaintances playing it. Intrigued, he learned its rules, and came to love the game. So much so, that he was sad when backgammon's popularity faded from view. Like a once-brilliant sun that dips below the horizon, Oby believed the game could, and should, win hearts and minds once more. It deserved to regain its glory, just as he also believed his Russian homeland deserved to regain its freedom and cast out its oppressors.

When the prince reached the age of forty-eight, he decided it was time to act on his belief. By this time, Backgammon was only a favorite of the upper crust, mainly within men's clubs in big cities. Therefore, if he were to make its sun rise again, he must start with them. He needed a great palace to stage a tournament for such players—not fought with lances and armor but contested with dice and pieces. A friend told him of such a "palace"—the new Lucaya Beach Hotel on Grand Bahama Island. It was there that Prince Oby would organize his tournament. This hotel, newly opened, was receptive to anything that would help advertise its existence. A gaming tournament seemed ideal.

Prince Obolensky knew that wealthy players would not mind bearing the expense of flying to the island. There would be gaiety, minstrels, and fair ladies in fine gowns. The romance of the tournament also appealed to reporters and photographers. Knowing that the wealthy liked the Bahamas' lure of legal gambling, Oby arranged for a bookmaker to handle the "gold" that would be bet on the contestants—as if they were, indeed, knights paired up in jousting duels.

Dozens of players signed up. Oby ran an auction to raise more prize money, then realized he needed a "Black Knight" for the crowd to both fear and revile. He convinced the self-proclaimed "world's best backgammon player" Bulgarian-born Nick Sergeant, who once almost bit off an opponent's ear after losing a game, to come and participate.

The Prince's tournament was a splendid affair with a happy ending. Exceptional players reached the finals. Sergeant—the Black Knight—was knocked out in the semis, to the joy of the audience. A young upstart named Porter Iiams defeated the favored player, Johnny Crawford. It was as if the Black Knight and Galahad the Pure were both beaten by a squire destined to become a great knight. The press gushed in its coverage.

"What happened after the tournament?" I ask the Gnome.

"To find out, we must go inside here." We've stopped walking at 65th and Park in front of a stately fourteen-story building. "This was once the Mayfair House Hotel." We enter the restaurant in the building; the Gnome informs me that, here, he will "go back" to 1978 and witness the opening of the Park 65 Backgammon Club.

"Will Oby be there?" I ask.

"No," the Gnome replies in a monotone. "Tim will be. Tim Holland held court here."

"I know who you mean! I once knew Tim Holland."

"Holland. Yes. Like Oby, Tim happened upon the game by chance, became energized by it, and during the 1970s took backgammon to never-seen heights, building upon the set-up by the Prince. Holland became the game's most flamboyant figure. A Showman who hardly ever lost a game in his prime."

I knew Tim Holland by way of Bob Reiss, with whom I had worked in the games business. Bob, a brilliant marketer and sales visionary, helped Holland build a crowd of backgammon players from all walks of life.

The Gnome is now zoned and narrating what he sees. "There is a lively cocktail party in progress. Very stylish people. Gowns with plunging necklines; black ties and tuxedos. Park 65 only admits players with serious backgammon skills.

Holland is its founder and president. I see him. He is seated next to his wife at the time, Lona. Quite attractive. Tim had four or five wives. And no lack of lady friends, I understand. He looks very dashing."

"I remember Tim as tall, well-groomed, and always dressed as if on his way to a photo shoot at GQ."

"His suit jacket has *real* buttonholes on its sleeves."

"He was also very confident, outgoing, bold."

"Not at this moment, Phil. Holland has the look of a murderer because the game he is playing is not going well. Luck is not his lady, so far. He is chain-smoking; a hazy white cloud hangs over his head. He doesn't notice; his eyes are riveted on the board. He shakes his dice cup. Ah, this roll is a good one."

I think back to my childhood when backgammon was merely the game whose array of isosceles triangles came

printed on the back of cheap, tortured chess boards. My childhood friends and I ignored it.

However, by 1972, I was not immune to the craze fer-
mented by Prince Obolensky and Tim Holland. I was playing
for an initial bet of a dollar and making as much money as I lost.
Backgammon is a gambling game and is often pulse-pound-
ing, thanks to the inclusion of a modern innovation—the
"doubling cube."

The basic idea of the game is to roll two dice and, according to the roll, advance one or more of your fifteen "men" that
begin the game scattered among the board's thirty triangles

(spaces or "points"). A double, like 3-3, allows you to move not two of the number rolled, but *four*.

Your aim is to advance them all into your opponent's Home Board (quadrant) and then whisk them off the board to safety.

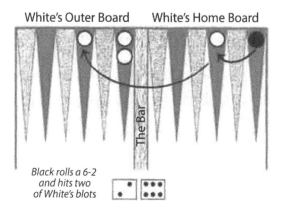

White's Outer Board   White's Home Board

The Bar

*Black rolls a 6-2
and hits two
of White's blots*

You control a "point" when at least two of your men occupy it. But a single man (a "blot") is vulnerable to being "hit" by an opposing man. If hit, your man comes off the board and must re-enter in the opponent's Home Board, being placed on a vacant point corresponding to one of the numbers of your roll. If the opponent occupies these points your man may not re-enter the board, and you forfeit your roll. *Ouch*.

You win the game if you get your last piece off the board before your opponent does. If you get all your men off before *any* of his escape, you've won a "gammon" (a double victory). Get them all off before he advances any one of his pieces into *your* home board, and you win a "backgammon" or quadruple victory.

Backgammon's surge in the '20s and '30s came about because of the introduction of the doubling cube, which ratcheted up the game's gambling appeal. The number on top is "turned" (doubled) to scare one's opponent into resigning—and paying up—before the game ends. The six sides of this special dice feature the numbers 2-4-8-16-32-64. A player may turn the cube to the next higher number and offer it to his opponent (typically when he has an advantage). If accepted, the stakes in the game have been "doubled" to the number showing. So, if you happen to be playing for a "dollar," any game in which the cube did not get "turned" would necessitate payment of that lowly dollar, or two dollars for a gammon victory or four dollars for a backgammon. But add in the impact of the cube and that innocent dollar mushrooms. A game redoubled six times (which is rare) reaches sixty-four dollars. Should such a game end in a backgammon, the payoff becomes $256 (a far cry from one dollar). Imagine risking a thousand dollars at the outset! You get it. Modern backgammon is gripping. Skill is essential to win often. But Lady Luck can sometimes obliterate skill.

The Gnome continues, "After a few more rolls, Tim has his opponent right where he wants him. Both players have only one more man to bring around and begin bearing off.

Tim cleverly gives his opponent a shot by leaving a blot. His opponent rolls. Oh dear, he hits the blot. Now Tim rolls and hits the piece hung out to dry by his opponent. The opponent rolls but fails to re-enter. It is now rather hopeless. Holland turns the Doubling Cube from four to eight and offers it to his opponent, who promptly declines it. Game over. Finally, Holland's death mask is lifted. He smiles and lights up yet another cigarette. He stands and accepts the applause of the crowd. The Showman is back in stride."

We regain Park Avenue. The Gnome leads me uptown as he continues the story of Prince Alexis Obolensky.

"After his first tournament at the Grand Bahama Hotel, Oby realized he could entice the greater public to embrace Backgammon if he gained the endorsement of celebrities. They were always in the news. So he left his career in Florida and moved to Los Angeles. One by one, he persuaded big names to play the game and be available for publicity photos. Stars like John Wayne, Grace Kelly, Sean Connery, Lucille Ball, and Jim Brown—the football player turned actor.

"One day, he persuaded the greatest hedonist of the era— Hugh Hefner, publisher of *Playboy Magazine*—to try the game. Hefner was galvanized."

"Bob Reiss and Tim were invited to play Hefner," I inform the Gnome. "By then, 'Hef' was a backgammon fanatic. Bob told me they arrived at midnight and found Hefner in his typical uniform—pajamas. He was keen to play all night long. Legend had it he once played for seventy-two hours straight. Hef began publishing backgammon stories in *Playboy*, including photo spreads of celebrities enjoying it with him at the Playboy mansion. The magazine's circulation was at its peak; men of all ages were reading it.

This "endorsement" by *Playboy* created acceptance from coast to coast, and across all income-earning age brackets. Other publications like *Time* and *Newsweek* soon picked up on the game. Tournaments cropped up everywhere. Oby founded a backgammon association and standardized the game's rules. He wrote three books on the game's play as well.

I continued. "Bob told me that Tim Holland boasted of never holding a real job. When younger, he tried to make a living by playing golf for high stakes. After a grueling match, he noticed two older golfers playing a table game in the clubhouse. He thought: *What is this?* Holland quickly learned how to play backgammon, and ditched golf.

"Tim would later claim to have lost thirty thousand dollars while figuring out its winning strategies, but thereafter he was destined to make more money than any backgammon player in history. He wrote books and endorsed backgammon sets made by Bob Reiss, whose company, Reiss Games, struck a deal with Tim to endorse a whole range of products (including a teaching device called AutoBackgammon). Backgammon went from selling twenty thousand sets per year to at least two million, perhaps as many as four million."

"Shades of Scrabble's rapid acceptance twenty years earlier," the Gnome mentions.

Prince Obolensky decided to retire in 1977, at the age of sixty-two. He had completed his quest. He did not worry that Backgammon would decline without him. Tim Holland held the spotlight.

We cross East 71st Street. I don't know who the Gnome is taking me to visit next, but I know we must be going to visit an expert who will tell us the wisdom imbued by this high-stakes game. Somewhat to my surprise, we re-enter Wally Zupan's building and the Gnome says to the doorman, "Wally's expecting us once more." He turns to me. "Remember, I told you Wally wasn't only a chess expert. He's a great backgammon player as well."

As we enter Wally's duplex, I discern the rattle of dice in a leather cup. The sound is coming from his library. I see Zupan seated at the table on his dais, playing backgammon with... Bob Reiss! I haven't seen Bob in ages. Despite advancing years and a head of gray hair, Bob looks just as athletic as when he ran Reiss Games. He was, after all, a former basketball star at Columbia. And his smile it still as broad as his shoulders.

Wally Zupan jumps up. "I hope you don't mind that I staged a reunion."

Bob and I embrace. I turn to the Gnome. "Did you know this in advance?"

The Gnome shakes his head. "No. Wally only said he'd have an associate present when we came by this time."

Bob Reiss

The four of us settle around the big table and talk backgammon. Wally and Bob resume their game, which is still young.

Wally says, "The history of this game is quite amazing. It goes back to the beginning when the Sumerian civilization flourished. There are written records of it, and ornate artifacts. It is quite possible the game was devised before mankind conceived writing. It reached Egypt seven centuries later. Boards were discovered in Kind Tut's tomb, from 1500 B.C. Advance a millennium and it is being played in Greece, and then in Rome where it gets the name 'Tables.' Roman paintings depict it, including a version where players bet their clothes and had to strip. Nero lost a fortune playing Tables. Of course, he wasn't very bright. By this time, the 'everyman' on the streets of Rome was playing the game. Go to Pompeii. You'll see wall paintings. The Romans took it to Great Britain and the English latched onto it. It then crossed the ocean with them. Thomas Jefferson became a fan. Somehow, the pre-Columbian Native Americans in Central America also got ahold of a version, which suggests Asians brought it when they migrated."

"But as you know, Phil," Bob adds, "None of this history meant squat until the cube appeared." Bob is smart, speaks plainly, and often lectures about his accomplishments.

I respond, "Ah, the doubling cube, the key to the game's juice. I understand it was invented in the 1920s. Do either of you know by whom?"

Reiss shakes his head, but Wally's smallish mouth grins. "I learned the answer a few years go. Too bad Oby wasn't around, because it seems the cube's inventor was another royal Russian. A fellow by the name of Grand Duke Dmitri. Believe it or not, he was the same Dmitri who helped murder Rasputin and he also contributed to the creation of Chanel No.5 perfume. I'm not kidding. He was romantically involved with Coco Chanel."

The Gnome asks a pertinent question. "Did this grand duke only invent the *idea* of doubling the stakes, or did he conceive of the idea and *apply* it to a cube?"

"Good point!" Wally responds. "Dmitri was the only member of his family to survive the communists. Like Oby, he spent time in Paris and dallied with Coco. Most probably, he came up with the idea of doubling the stakes in backgammon, with her, in Paris. That he originated the doubling idea is not in dispute. Written proof of that has been found. But it remains unclear who took his idea and slapped it on the six sides of a cube. Perhaps he did himself, perhaps not."

"Well, it would make sense to do that," Bob says. "You've got four dice, why not add a fifth?"

"What can you tell us about Tim Holland that I may not know?" I ask Bob.

Bob replies, "For starters, he was great with crowds. I took him to Chicago to introduce our new line. He was fabulous. Publicity always followed Tim, which made it easy for me to sell in a lot of games to the majors [largest retailers]. And he liked women. One of his ex-wives married Johnny Carson."

The Gnome steers the conversation. "Phil and I have this premise that all great games impart wisdom, otherwise they would disappear. So what does backgammon impart?"

Bob has just rolled a double six, which provides him a clear advantage on the board. He offers Wally the cube at "2." While Zupan ponders, Bob takes a crack at the answer.

"I think the appeal of Backgammon is so great because it's for everybody. You don't need to gamble big money. You can play for pennies or just for sport. That's important because the lessons the game teaches also connect with the hoi polloi, not just the rich and famous."

"So what would be an example?" I ask.

"Here's the first. Getting a good or a bad start in life doesn't determine how your life will end up. Take me. I grew up in the projects in Brooklyn, went to a high school where it was said, when you graduated, you either went to college or became a criminal. I didn't have the means to go to college on my own, but a guy from Columbia saw me play basketball and offered me a full scholarship. I tell you, I worked my tail off in appreciation."

Wally has decided to accept the cube. He looks up and adds, "In backgammon, if you fall behind, you switch to a back game. That's what I must do now. I will purposely try not to advance my pieces and then hit one of Bob's blots while he's bearing off. If I control most of the points in his home board, he'll likely not be able to re-enter. Then I will run."

This is similar to what Holland did in the game the Gnome visualized him playing.

"Here's another one," Bob says as he rolls a 5-4 and leaves a blot, albeit one unlikely to be hit. "The game may look like a game of chance, but it's filled with strategy and precision. You don't get far in life if you are imprecise or sloppy. In this game, you have to know the right move for every combination of the dice, in all circumstances. That's precision. For example, knowing the exact odds that you'll be hit if you leave a blot. Here's another: you need to look ahead. Don't just live for the moment. You should always figure out what could happen on your next turn. If you do this in real life, you won't be caught flat-footed so much. Make your decisions based on solid facts and good intuition. Don't go by emotion."

"What if you're not money-driven? How do you benefit?"

"Look," Bob replies, "Being content, developing good relationships, having integrity—they are all priceless. But even if these are your goals, it still pays to lower the odds of chance preventing you from realizing them. You need income."

"I have another," the Gnome interjects. "To quote Yogi Berra, 'It ain't over 'til it's over.'"

"How true," says Wally, as he rolls perfectly and hits the blot Bob left him. "Do not count your chickens, or your blessings, until the final score is tallied." He offers the cube back to Bob turned to "4."

Bob looks at it, reads the gleam in Wally's eyes and says, "No thanks."

"I think I psyched him out," Wally opines.

"Not so," says Bob. "I got no safety net in this game. I don't think I can come back. In real life, I always had a back-up plan. I learned young to tuck money away in case things got tough. I built up cash to start my business. I was frugal. It paid off. Going into hock or playing All-or-Nothing is a fool's game."

We relax and toss back a beer. I find myself catching up on old times with Bob while the Gnome and Wally chat about stock tips and the price of gold. When we wrap up, Wally suggests we raise our glasses for a toast. "I wish Oby and Tim could be with us today. Let's toast the prince of backgammon and the game's greatest showman."

The Prince passed away in New York City at the age of seventy-one in 1986.

Emphysema claimed the Showman in Florida during 2010. Tim was seventy-nine.

CHAPTER TEN

TO PLAY OR NOT TO PLAY

I'm winded by the time we get back from Reykjavik. Although we've undertaken nine trips, the Gnome is keen to keep going. I call a temporary halt. Besides, something that came up in Iceland caused a memory to surface and gnaw at me. I reveal this to the Gnome. He advises therapy. *Why not?*

The following evening, we're leaning on the rail of the back deck, absorbing the placid scene outside Gloucester Harbor. The lighthouse is blinking, gulls are floating on currents of air, sails are coming about to catch the breeze. "Let's take a load off," I suggest.

We ease ourselves onto recliners.

My wife, Anna, appears and sets down a big pitcher of sangria on ice, with lemon slices and pineapple chunks. "This should help you two to relax." She fills two big glasses and hands one to each to us. I catch a glimpse of her studying me intently as her light hair dances in the breeze.

"Yes?"

"Well, I just wanted to see if I still recognize you. I've seen so little of you lately."

"My apologies," the Gnome offers. "Epic adventures take time. Will you join us?"

Anna senses the Games Gnome is being polite; she makes an equally polite excuse to go shopping.

The Gnome sits up, swings his legs towards me, and plants his sandals on the deck. "Do you want to tell me what's distracting you?"

The flavored wine is working its magic. I unburden. "You said something when we were paying our respects to the late Bobby Fischer. You mentioned that most of those tortured cardboard chessboards whose purchase he stimulated were never used. They gathered dust on shelves in oh-so-many homes."

"Why would that fact bother you, Phil?"

"On the surface, it doesn't. Fischer created a crowd and a lot of people impulsively went out and bought a chess set to prove they were part of the crowd. I get that. But that in turn caused me to gnaw on a bigger morsel of doubt. And I remembered something disturbing about Ernest Dichter."

The Gnome strokes his beard and screws up his face. I wonder if he is about channel Freud. *("Vhat have vee got he-eh? Vhat ist your prob-leem?")* Instead, he says, "Hmm. Start by talking about doubt, Phil."

"It won't make sense out of context. Its roots run deep."

"Then go back and dig at those roots."

By now, I'm uninhibited and delighted to try to dig up the roots below the doubt. "It all begins with the makers of tortured cardboard. The companies who made most of the games we've analyzed, like Parker Brothers and Selchow & Righter. She here goes…"

Many, many years ago, the "Hats"—a firm's owners and managers—employed quite a lot of "Make-Its"—the folks who actually tortured the cardboard and put the games together. They also needed a few "Bright Eyes" who styled new games, rendered artwork for them, and made sure the rules were well-written. Of course, there were also Drummers—salesmen who sold the games, but they didn't hang around the factory; they were expected to be on the road. All of these folks felt part of a family, so squabbles, bickering, and laughter was expected and taken in stride.

The Hats made sure the bills were paid and encouraged the Drummers to look for new business so the Make-Its could keep busy. The money was kept in a big bag with a dollar sign on it.

Every now and then—one never knew when—a carrier pigeon would come home to roost and it would bring word of a new game out there. The Hats would go investigate and if they liked this game, they said to the Bright Eyes and Make-Its, "We took some money out of the bag to purchase a new game for you to design and manufacture."

The Make-Its and Bright Eyes asked, "What is the name of this new game?" And the Hats would reply, "It is called Monopoly" (or Scrabble or Clue or Risk or…whatever).

More often, however, the pigeon's note read, "I have a new game idea," and it was signed by some would-be game inventor. The Hats would usually send back a note back reading: "Thanks, but no thanks." But on occasion, they might write, "We'd like to talk about it." These games had names like Derby Day, Pirate and Traveler, Little Noddy's Taxi, and Port-of-Call—none of which anyone had ever heard of, especially if there had been no chaos to inspire their creation. Operating on a hunch, the Hats would sometimes take money out of the bag and publish one of these. If, by chance, the Drummers got a lot of orders and this new game attracted a crowd, everyone was busy and happy for some time to come. But if not, well, some of the Make-Its and Bright Eyes would be looking for work elsewhere.

"What does this mean to you?" the Gnome asks.

"It simply means," I tell him, "that way back when, in the 1930s, forties and fifties, the toy and game business was very dependent on luck. The notion of creating a hit game according to some specification hadn't come about."

"Tell me about trying to make hit games on demand."

"That notion started in the 1960s when big consumer product companies like General Mills looked at game companies like Parker Brothers and decided that, if *they* were the Hats, their finely-honed systems could be installed to shape up a games business and make it grow by a steady fifteen percent each and every year."

"Ah, systems. Talk about systems."

I do so. By the time I was hired at Parker Brothers—located in Beverly, Massachusetts—General Mills had owned the firm for a decade and it had many new categories of employees, each similar to a counterpart at General Mills in Minneapolis, Minnesota. Foremost amongst them were the Marketing Minds. There were also the Financial Fiends—they were all actually quite nice and more often called "Bean Counters." They minded the bag of money for General Mills. There was also a department called Human Resources and its guys and gals were known as the Mother Hens.

"Were there Make-Its and Bright Eyes?"

"They were still there, of course. Parker Brothers needed lots and lots of Make-Its because it sold far more games in the seventies than it had in the fifties."

"How did this new system work?"

I explain. The Bean Counters made sure everyone had a budget and stuck to it. There was to be no money for whims. Reports were generated weekly by the Great IBM 360 Computer—which occupied a spacious room of its own, complete with air conditioning. These reports alerted the Hats if budgets were being minded or not and if the Drummers had gotten enough orders or not. The Mother Hens devised benefits, pay levels, incentives, and workplace policies intended to treat everyone fairly and prevent bickering and squabbles. Laughter was to be appropriate, not excessive. Most importantly, the Marketing Minds—armed with lots and lots of industry data and research—would tell our "Oracle at Delphi"—the Great IBM 360—what they knew and the Great Machine would print out plans and projections that the Marketing Minds would show to the Bright Eyes and—like doctors with an irrefutable diagnosis in hand—pronounce something like, "There are going to be more seven-year-olds next year, therefore you must make for us a new board game these youngsters will love and beg their mothers to buy." The leaders of the Bright Eyes were told to communicate other needs to inventors who awaited insight in order to torture cardboard correctly. There would be no waiting around for the carrier pigeons to come home to roost. Meanwhile, the Bright Eyes would create whatever new games the outside inventors could not come up with, blessed by the awesome insight from the Oracle. I should add that Parker Brothers was just one of many companies that relied on Marketing Minds backed by an Oracle to compose wise and perceptive guidance. If you had coughed up two or three million on a mainframe computer, how could any firm ignore its advice?

"Are we getting closer to the cause of your doubt?"

"Indeed," I reply. "The Research Boys."

"Talk about…"

I cut him off. I'm already on topic. The Research Boys (and they were all of the male persuasion back then) had lots of tools and money from the Bag to provide the right input for our Oracle. For example, they relied on NPD (National Panel Diary) to discover what quantities consumers had purchased of individual games among all game companies.

They built up quite a log of tapes and photos.

*The castle-like Institute of Motivational
Research building and Ernest Dichter*

Most especially, they were well-versed in Ernest Dichter's
bag of analytical tricks and organized in-depth focus groups
to probe consumers (typically young mothers) and learn what
they thought about this or that idea, this or that color, and
how much they would pay for the ideas and the colors. They
also subscribed to special studies from marketing organizations
like the Research Council and they organized play testing of

each and every new game to make sure its rules were comprehendible and easy to read (the latter proved invaluable, not so much the others).

"It sounds like they thought of everything," the Gnome says. I detect a devilish gleam in his eyes. "No more chance, every new game purposeful and perfected. What could go wrong?"

I laugh. "Everything. Naturally, it didn't work. The toy and game business is a fashion-like business; it doesn't make necessities like toothpaste or breakfast cereal. The personnel systems, the good financial controls, and the platoons of young well-educated executives—they were excellent. And the Marketing Minds were really smart and had very good intent; they truly believed they could produce immortal games without chaos or chance."

"But didn't the firm grow a lot during your years there and thereafter? Something must have worked."

I chuckle. "Sure. The carrier pigeons hadn't been retired. Every now and then, one of them would come back with a note reading, "I was traumatized by chaos, and came up with a great game idea you've never thought of." And if the head of the Bright Eyes was intrigued, he or she would check it out. And sure enough, while the IBM 360 had never inspired a plan that included anything like this idea, the Marketing Minds were smart enough to admit it was the future—and the Bean Counters took some money out of the Bag so the idea could be purchased and the Bright Eyes made it look really good. The Marketing Minds then devised brilliant TV commercials to attract the Crowd and the gung-ho Drummers sold lots of it. The Make-Its, of course, were kept very busy."

"And there was plenty upon the land." The Gnome helps himself to another glass of the red stuff. "Pardon me, Phil, but where's your angst? Why would this bother you? Sure, the new systems did not contemplate the whims of the games business, but ultimately, those platoons of young professionals knew how to apply their talents once a hit was in hand."

I set down my glass and clear my throat. "Along the way, the Research Boys periodically asked people a lot of questions about games and about their preferences. You know, basic stuff, like: Do you play games and, if so, what kind? Whom do you play with? What do you like about playing games? And they made sure the results were shared with the Bright Eyes, like me."

"Want to talk about it?" I felt as though I were sitting with a psychoanalyst.

"The Research Boys told us they concluded, for a fact, that half of the people can't bring themselves to play games. And of those who do play games, half don't play to win, so…"

The Gnome interrupts. "Ah, those folks play for the camaraderie, the social pleasure. That is the way it should be. No harm in that."

"But there was harm. The Marketing Minds took as gospel what the Research Boys reported and told the Bright Eyes: Forget about immortality. We need games to satisfy our fifteen percent growth target next year. Give us immediacy, and we'll give you labels to slap on top of whimsy. Go with it!"

"Label slaps?"

I explain that "label slapping" means exploiting a license from a movie, book, or TV show, by applying it to a quickly-devised game. Maybe the label is Star Wars, or a Marvel Comic character, or the latest fantasy-themed novel. Whatever, it was fully expected that the game version would sell for one year, two with any luck, and then the Make-Its would be told not to put together any more; another label slap was coming.

"Okay, so the Marketing Minds took advantage of hot trends. You said yourself, games are a fashion-oriented business. Problem?"

I sit up and motion for the Gnome to recline. It is my turn to play therapist. Facing him, I say, "Relaxed? Good. Talk about great games and chaos."

"The birth of a great game is stimulated by chaotic times."

"Talk about chance."

"A game born in chaos survives by chance, and—I know where you're going Phil. Only truly great games impart wisdom and live forever."

"So how, Mr. Gnome, can you create the next great game at a company that spends all its time on fads and label-slapping?"

"You might," he replies, raising a knowing finger, "because, while the company is preoccupied with its own myopic vision, somewhere out there may be an inventor who is shocked into action by chaos beyond the influence of a Great Oracle."

He hits the nerve: there is no perfection in the games business. It takes a good systematized company to produce a great game *once it arises*. It takes a great company with means to attract the Crowd. But ever since the birth of the American game industry, no company has created its own game hit without the spark of an inventor residing someplace else.

The Gnome, still reclined, contemplates, "There is something gnawing at me as well. A long time ago, I learned something disturbing about the habits of game players. I gleaned that many players rely too much on intuition or whim when making a decision in a game. Most players don't think logically and that suggests they analyze their real-life decisions with improper care."

"Go on."

"I believe in applying intuition, but selectively and only if it is finely honed. That talent can take years of experience to develop. But chance is a losing proposition. I'm reminded of friends who routinely burn up ten to twenty percent of their take-home pay each week buying lottery tickets. Such games of chance are fixed. While many people feed them, very few are fed by them. Do you know why this disturbs me, Phil?"

I don't flinch. "Wisdom imparted without pain by the great games goes under-appreciated by the many."

The Gnome nods and becomes philosophical. "I have always felt I could lead a renaissance in belief in games and their benefit." He stands up and admires the pink glow on the horizon; the sun has just set. "An Enlightenment. It has not been easy."

"I admire your faith in games."

He sighs. "I am glad we had this talk."

"Where from here?" I ask the Gnome.

"The games we have looked at so far, like Monopoly, Parcheesi, and Chess, are solid examples of tortured cardboard, like the trunk of a tree. Now we are going to investigate great games that challenge the notion of tortured cardboard. Much tougher to wrap your mind around, because each is like a branch: it doesn't grow upwards, it grows out and spreads."

My wife returns; we dine at our favorite local restaurant. Satiated, the Gnome insists we play three-handed Canasta to cap off the evening. "If this were a board game, I'd take you to South America where it began," he remarks, laying down his cards and winning the first hand. "Life is good."

CHAPTER ELEVEN

CAN TORTURED CARDBOARD THINK?

After our respite, I find myself opening a car door two hundred miles away, stretching my legs in the parking lot of the J House Hotel in Greenwich, Connecticut. The Gnome hands me a postcard. "This is what it looked like when the guys from IBM descended here back in 1961; it was then named the New Englander Motor Hotel." My eyes take in the card, then the building. Its gray walls were originally a cherry red; its dark roof once white. Yes, there have been alterations. But the resemblance is still unmistakable.

We go inside; another friendly face behind a front desk greets the Gnome; we are led to a large conference room. "It happened in here," this fellow says reverently, as if he is a minister and we are treading on hallowed ground. He turns on the overhead lights and closes the door as he leaves. The room looks like a classroom: rows of long tables and chairs, a whiteboard at the far end. The Gnome is already "back then."

"I see a commanding-looking fellow cajoling a large group of men, all dressed alike. White shirts and dark ties. Their hair is neatly trimmed and most are wearing glasses. Some are sitting; some are standing against the walls and fidgeting. There is tension; I do not think things are going well."

"What's the fellow's name?"

"Hold on. A tall guy leaning against the wall calls out 'Gene,' and offers a suggestion. The leader nods and scrawls on the blackboard, which is nearly filled with chalked words and numbers. A baby-faced guy, sitting with hands folded as if in prayer, calls out meekly, "Mister Amdahl, I...I think we do have to replace our entire digital line with a system. However painful." Amdahl cleans his glasses before speaking. The gap of silence gains everyone's attention."

"Gene Amdahl? I know that name. There was a computer company named Amdahl in the eighties and nineties."

"Same guy, apparently. But in this motel, Gene first makes his mark. He is pointing at the timid guy. 'Quint, thank you. Listen up everybody. We've been here for three weeks and we now know we must kill every computer IBM has ever made. The mission of SPRED is to point our company not only towards the near future, but the *deep* future. Accept it. We need to design a unified *system* of computers and peripherals, from smallest to biggest, all working together; all need to run on the same software. We've got two and half years to pull it off. Now, maybe some of you aren't up to it. So let me have a show of hands. Who's on board?'" The Gnome seems to freeze; nothing further is coming out of his mouth.

"What's happening? How did the vote go?"

The Gnome comes around. "Sorry, big moment. Unanimous. Amdahl just told these guys that, if they pull it off, they would by credited with the biggest idea ever in computers. The group is buzzing. All are excited—I am excited just watching. They're already calling it the IBM System 360—meaning the full circle system."

I let this sink in. Inside this motel all those years ago, an engineering manager named Gene Amdahl led a team that developed the modern mainframe computer. The Gnome informs me that during the next twenty-five years, the "360" system will generate five hundred billion in business for IBM.

Five hundred *billion*. A math-savvy game player once put this in perspective. A billion seconds ago, you were thirty-two years younger (or maybe just a gleam, if your parents were still kids). A billion hours ago, was the Stone Age. I am impressed by IBM's vision and achievement, but wonder about its game relevance, so I challenge the Gnome. "What's the connection? How does the IBM 360 relate to tortured cardboard?"

"Phil…Phil. Twofold: the entire idea of 'systems' and also the realization that products can think. As the world in the sixties fills with thinking machines, intelligence will be applied to more and more products. 'Why cannot games also think?' will become a hot question. The century-long progression of unique and unrelated board games is about to be turned upside down. What's wrong with lines of games—with similar rules? Why not embrace *systems* of games, just like all the IBM gadgets that work together as one happy family?"

I get it. "If IBM computers can think and make logical decisions, why can't games go from 'roll-the-dice-and-draw-a-card' amusements to mathematically solid contests where the real world is emulated and thoughtful decisions are rewarded?"

"Right. 'I think,' says the game, 'therefore I am tortured cardboard.'"

"Gnomie, you must be pleased to have witnessed the birth of a new kind of chaos that would shake up board games."

The Gnome pulls on imaginary suspenders. "I feel like a proud father."

"I was swept up in this, you know. Many of us believed we could make cardboard think."

"Phil, go back to the beginning."

I tell the Gnome what I recollect. Before 1962, game companies had produced unique games; each had to be different from the last or be derided as a "knock-off." At this time, the first true line of thinking games coalesced inside a little company in Baltimore, Maryland, named Avalon Hill. "AH" began to offer a line of "simulation" games—games whose play and themes were accurate replicas of real-life activities— be it running a business ("Management"), driving a racecar ("Le Mans"), or waging a legal battle ("Verdict"). However, their most popular games were recreations of famous battles—games such as "Gettysburg," "D-Day," "Stalingrad," and "Waterloo." All of these battle games shared similar rules and gameplay procedures.

Moreover, Avalon Hill exploited tortured cardboard to its fullest. Their games didn't include plastic pieces. Rather, flat die-cut cardboard "counters" printed with military symbols served as playing pieces. The only plastic part found in each of their games was a simple die, used to provide a random outcome to battles ("weighted" according to the relative size of each force). The information printed on their counters was essential to gameplay.

But Avalon Hill faltered and was taken over in bankruptcy proceedings by its two largest creditors—a box maker and a printing company. Both were adept at fabricating cardboard. Avalon Hill had been the brainchild of Charles R. Roberts. In 1953, he was in the coast guard where he developed an interest in military history and soon devised his first game—"Tactics"—to further his understanding of military strategy. He applied many of the techniques of historical strategists who had served the great powers in Europe and Asia—and whose ideas were refined by the general staff of the U.S. Army. Charles Roberts is now rightfully acclaimed as the father of thinking board games.

Back in 1958, Roberts launched an improved version of his initial game ("Tactics II") along with a new one named

"Gettysburg." He thought these two would be his only war-games. He began to add non-military games to his line, which found acceptance by more and more retailers. At the same time, a court ruling deemed it illegal for manufacturers to set retail prices, whereupon many under-capitalized "discounters" popped up across the country. Several purchased Roberts' games. Competition became keen. Many couldn't pay their bills and went bankrupt, which caused a crisis among their suppliers, Roberts' firm included. When he failed to collect the money he owed Avalon Hill, he lost everything.

"What were the names of his creditors?" the Gnome asks.

"Smith Paper Box Company and Monarch Printing. They took over Avalon Hill and kept just one employee: an ex-advertising executive named Tom Shaw. A good guy. Shaw realized that the only AH games with a devoted following were its wargames. So during the next several years, Shaw—on a tight budget—would publish two new war games per annum. Young adult males who loved the excitement of recreating historical battles devoured each new game as it appeared and clamored for more. Shaw did not have the freedom to respond. It was during this 'hunger' period that I founded Gamescience Corporation—I might add with Shaw's support and enthusiasm. He benefited from an outlet to quench some of his customers' thirst.

Charles Roberts   **Tom Shaw**

"By the early seventies, there were many new publishers of military simulations, like historian Jim Dunnigan's Simulations Publications. I worked with Jim for a while."

The Gnome observes, "The category of thinking games quickly narrowed itself down to wargames only, but countless titles began to appear."

"True. Their makers began to look under the carpet, so to speak, to find more and more historical battles to emulate. But, in my opinion, they all missed the big point."

"Which was?"

"The market was passionate, but too narrow. If you weren't a geek, that is to say a brainy male between the ages of twelve and thirty, these complicated, tedious games held no appeal, despite the thrill of rewriting history by playing them."

"As I see it, the notion of thinking games was solid. But folks could not afford to put an IBM 360 in the basement. So all this 'thinking' had to be manual. The so-called simulation of real life relied on complicated numerical charts, lengthy booklets filled with intricate rules—like where you could and could not move on a turn—and military symbolism that would make even a soldier's head spin. No offense."

"But somehow, this narrow market morphed and would explode a decade or so later."

"True! What happened came out of left field. It is a story unto itself. I am saving it for later." The gnome makes a request, "Tell me again how you got into the games business."

"I got hooked on Avalon Hill games while in high school, even though few of my classmates were up for them. This didn't deter me; I began to invent my own. I paid fifty dollars for a spirit duplicator and began to print copies of my first wargame. Thanks to the friendship I made with Tom Shaw, I had access to names and addresses of kids like myself who were into these games. I convinced fifty of them to buy the paper kits I produced. I assigned each purchaser a country of the world or world area. The idea was for them to form two grand alliances and wipe out the other team. It was a play-by-mail game."

"Play by mail. I remember those days. Can you describe it?"

"All communication and moves were written down and sent by mail."

"Must have taken forever!"

"Nobody seemed to mind back then. To simulate dice rolls, players consulted the stock market pages. The final volume digit for a stock like IBM represented the number rolled."

"A year or two later, you stuck your neck out and started a company."

"I founded Gamescience Corporation with money I really needed for college. My confidence was blind and sky-high. What did I know? Like Alfred Butts, I ordered nicely boxed copies of my first game. I ran my little company from college, while my family back east handled the assembly and shipment. In retrospect, it was a crazy thing to do. But it got me into the games business and eventually helped pay for my education. I attended the annual Hobby Show during my junior year. A New York-based toy and hobby firm took notice and offered to buy Gamescience; I made a modest profit and agreed to work for them after I graduated.

"When college ended, Anna and I got married and moved to Queens. On my first day of work, my boss told me, 'Your simulation games are nice but we're never going to make enough money on them. The market is too small.' So I shifted gears and began to invent games with mass market potential. I worked for a couple of other small game firms too; we made some pretty nifty non-war, adult-level games. It worked out."

"Beyond your adventures, the Big Guys took note and decided, 'Why not make wargames a mass-market success?'"

"Parker and Milton Bradley tried. During the centennial of the War Between the States, Parker Brothers hooked up with

Life magazine and jointly introduced a new wargame entitled '1863.' Parker published the boxed version; *Life* magazine printed the rules, gameboard, and pieces in the pages of one of its issues. Readers were encouraged to cut these out and glue them to cardboard to make a playable game. At the same time, Milton Bradley began to publish wargames with plastic ships, airplanes, and soldiers. Games like 'Broadsides' and 'Dogfight.' These sold okay and, eventually, Milton Bradley acquired the very successful Second World War game named 'Axis & Allies®' which also had lots of plastic pieces. It still sells."

"If anything enduring came out of this era, it was the collective wisdom imparted by all these simulations, especially wargames."

I agree. "From the time I first played Gettysburg, I realized you needed to learn certain military principles in order to win. These were fundamental. Fighting a battle on a gameboard rubbed off on how I approached real-life conflict."

"Hold that thought." The Gnome motions; we return to the car. "We are going to drive to the other side of the state," he advises. "Wait 'til you hear what my wise friend Tim Grell has to say."

Our knock is answered by a husky man. His appearance is a bit jarring. He is dressed in a gray robe, cinched at the waist. His feet are clad in white socks and brown sandals. A graying beard hides his chin and obscures his lips. His face betrays no emotion. His black hair is pulled back in a ponytail. The "devil's horns" area of his hairline had receded, giving him a sinister appearance, but I quickly realize that is misleading. His placid blue eyes are framed by delicate wire rims and he speaks in a soft voice as he extends a warm hand. "I'm Grell. Follow me."

We descend into his basement and find ourselves in an alternate reality, or so it seems. We stand in a very large, well-lit room given over to rows of floor-to-ceiling bookshelves made of birch. They are loaded with wargames. The Gnome says, "Grell has every one ever made, or so he thinks." I notice an original Tactics I game by Avalon Hill (only two thousand were made; most were destroyed). He's got my first game too, Viet Nam (only five hundred of the first edition were made).

Grell leads us to a gaming table at the center of his "world." A pot of tea awaits along with three hand-fired cups that look like they were forged a thousand years ago in China or Japan. In the center of the table is set out a large gameboard picturing ancient China. Dozens of small playing pieces in three different colors are positioned upon it; battles are in progress; Tim Grell seems to have assumed the roles of all three warring factions.

The Gnome offers some background as we sit. "When younger, Grell was an accountant and also a passionate wargamer, as you might suspect. He cleverly applied the savvy he learned from wargames to advance in his occupation. Eventually, he founded his own accounting firm. It grew large. Two years ago, he turned over management to his sons and retired. He can afford to do what he wants these days."

Grell chooses not to comment on the Gnome's introduction, as if it were an unnecessary waste of time. He remains soft-spoken, which pulls you closer to him—an effective means to garner attention.

"To play wargames well, it is advised to study Sun Tzu. He is the father of military thinking. What he recorded in *The Art of War* during the fifth century B.C. is as applicable today as it was during his lifetime. In fact, many modern generals have profitably applied his book's teachings. For example, the North Vietnamese leaders relied on them during the Vietnam conflict. Schwarzkopf and Powell used them to advantage in the First Gulf War. At a young age, I realized that wargames inculcate the wisdom of his principles. I learned to apply them to my life. I became successful."

"What are these principles?" the Gnome asks.

"Application of force should never be the beginning point of a venture. You will unnecessarily arouse opposition; your opponent will fight with greater conviction. One must realize that victory and defeat are psychological states. While you may, in fact, ultimately destroy your opponent, this is made easier if you maneuver first and unsettle his mental composure."

"And generate chaos, right Grell?" the Gnome offers helpfully.

He nods solemnly. "Yes. Your goal must be to instill chaos in the opposition's condition. When harmony exists, the opposition is unified. When disharmony is present, chaos often results in defeat. Or in decline, at the very least."

"Phil and I have spent several weeks investigating chaotic periods in history that led to great games being created."

"A military leader thinks in terms of terrain, weather, position, and timing. Every well-honed wargame I have ever played relies on quantifying these factors. But there is another: *morale*. In society, chaos caused by failing institutions or unyielding pressure by an external force threatens to undermine its entire value system. When one realizes his surrounding world is crumbling, restrained impulses sometimes burst forth and consume a person's mind. Ironically, this person is suddenly freed of restraint. Great ideas may follow." Grell pours himself another cup of tea.

"Do you have, perhaps, a short list of lessons taught by wargaming?" I ask.

He wastes no time expounding. "First, pick your battles; it's not wise to contest everything that bothers you. Next, act when conditions are favorable. Third, know your opposition better than you know yourself; otherwise he will surprise and thwart you. Fourth, have a solid plan, but don't reveal it. Accept that events seldom proceed according to plan; therefore, one must embrace change. Change leads to unexpected solutions, provided your mind and eye are sharp."

The Gnome contributes to this thought. "Opportunities can multiply. Once you find initial success in life, it will be easier to seize the next opportunity and make that a success. It's the equivalent of building an impressive resume; adding to your skillsets; benefiting from a positive reputation."

I offer this, "I don't think it is wise to remain in conflict for too long. Long-drawn-out conflict is draining. You should break off the battle and let go, especially when you're in a protracted stalemate."

Grell wraps this up with a ribbon. "Putting off solving a vexing problem inevitably results in a waste of time and money to fix it later, like a leaky roof." He lowers his head and places his hands on his knees. We sense the end of our visit.

The Gnome says, "Thank you, Tim Grell, for sharing what you learned from your wargames."

Grell's eyes light up behind his wire rims; a pleasant sound emanates from his throat. He gestures towards the gameboard. "Stay seated, gentlemen. You will notice that I am in the midst of a battle whose aim is the unification of China during the second century. You will further notice that three armies are engaged. I have brought the conflict to a time of great tension and excitement." Grell now strikes, in a manner of speaking. "We will play this game together from now on. You will assume the leadership of the green and blue forces, and I will battle you with the red."

"Is this a long game to play?" the Gnome asks.

Grell is already making Red's next move. "Hours. Not to worry. You will be well fed. My wife will bring takeout when she comes home from work this evening."

Chapter Twelve

AN UNHOLY MARRIAGE

We're standing across from a big gritty factory on Jamaica Avenue in Hollis, Queens, New York. I suspect the Gnome is once again pulling a prank on me, because he knows I used to work inside this building when it was the headquarters and main plant of the Ideal Toy Corporation—at the time, the nation's third largest maker of toys, dolls, and games.

"Does it look much different than when you worked here?"

"Not really. I'd say the main difference appears to be that several companies now share its five stories. Ideal filled its entirety." Time has weathered the facade of this massive building, but there's also a new "greenhouse" roof over the sixth floor "penthouse" and a beefier main entrance.

"Rough neighborhood, I'd say." The Gnome is looking around at the pedestrians walking along the sidewalk and the debris scattered about by an overturned trashcan.

"Hollis was a scary place when Ideal employed me. We were told never to walk alone, especially on winter evenings when it grew dark before closing time. But no one I knew was mugged, just some petty thefts. If you noticed something missing, like your hubcaps, you'd go across the street to Jerry's gas station and, amazingly, they'd be hanging on the wall and you could buy 'em back. Jerry thought he was doing us a favor by providing a marketplace of sorts."

"What else do you remember?"

"Employee parking was in remote lots, and you'd have to walk two blocks along the front of the building in order to get to the main entrance. In cold weather, a breeze would roll down from Hillside Avenue until it smacked into the building. With nowhere to go but sideways, it would compress and become a strong wind—almost hurricane force at times. Very biting in winter. I was glad to get inside and hear the hiss of the steam radiators."

"Why did Ideal hire you, Phil?"

"Well, Ideal—a major doll and toy company—was also the leader in plastic action games. However, it had tried and failed to make a go in cardboard games. They decided to try again and hired me because of my track record in board games.

It proved formidable. I had to set up the new board game division and figure out how to compete with the two giants, Parker Brothers and Milton Bradley. I had success, so the Hats decided I should run the action game division as well."

"What was Ideal's biggest-selling action game?"

"Mouse Trap®, which was a hybrid game. Its board was made from tortured cardboard and there was a bunch of plastic parts which, when inserted on the board, formed a 'Rube Goldberg' contraption whose aim was to trap the mouse-shaped playing pieces, one by one, when they reached the end of the printed path."

The Gnome eyes me sagaciously. "That is why we are here, Phil. I'm going back to the day of chaos when cardboard and plastic were first married in the board game business. Thirteen years before you started to work here."

"The purists called it a shotgun wedding. An unholy marriage. Others, like myself, accepted that cardboard could not continue to drive board game sales unless wedded to technology. In the 1960s, the use of plastics was exploding in many industries. It was logical to make use of it in board games. Inevitable."

I have mixed feelings as we re-enter the building. I follow the Gnome past security to the freight elevator that once lifted me to my fourth-floor office. It still groans and clanks on its way. When we emerge, I try not to register the new surroundings; I don't want my memories tainted.

A nice lady, working for a warehouse company, shows us to the old executive conference room, which is now used for storage. (Quite a shock.) The Gnome takes a deep breath and closes his eyes. He's going back. The idea for Mouse Trap was first presented to Ideal Toy in 1962. I heard the stories when

I arrived, because most of the people responsible were still working there. Ideal had a family mentally. You didn't quit the family.

Speaking of families, I vividly recall the excitement shared by my two sisters when they saw Mouse Trap on TV for the first time. One of them got it as a birthday present. They loved playing it, just to see the contraption capture their mice. They really didn't care who won.

The Gnome's voice drones on as he describes what he is now seeing. He brings to life the stories I was told. It is easy for me to fit these pieces into the larger story, which goes like this:

The power of Ideal resided in the molding department on its ground floor. It hummed with the deafening noise of eighty giant machines that liquefied plastic pellets and forced them under tremendous pressure into machined steel molds. Their cavities filled with the viscous material before water cooling hastened its hardening. The two halves of the steel mold separated, and the plastic parts came out. This process was endlessly repeated, as often as three times per minute.

But despite this powerful and unique investment in plastics to make toys, hobby kits, and doll parts, Ideal decided in 1960 that it would enter the game business to make *cardboard* games, whose components and packaging had to be sourced from external vendors. Why? Because the notion of plastic games hadn't popped up yet (a few novelty games aside, like the Bettye-B Company's vacuum-formed gameboard in the prior decade).

This attempt to establish a cardboard game business failed. Ideal lacked the finesse, savvy, and know-how to compete against game companies who'd been perfecting their skills for decades. Their one modest success was a clunky toy-game named "Haunted House," which looked like the vertical facade of a "spooky house." Plastic pegs served as playing pieces and were inserted into holes on the vertical game board to keep them in place. The mansion purposely looked like the one featured in the popular *Addams Family* television series. There was an owl-themed spinner rather than dice. Spring-loaded panels opened and revealed creepy objects. The game looked exciting in its TV commercial, but once kids got it home, they found its play was underwhelming. "Just a few bells and whistles, and otherwise the same play as a flat game board," my game inventor friend, Rene Soriano once said. "There was no interaction. B-o-r-i-n-g."

The disappointment of Haunted House, coupled with Ideal's failure to establish a board game line, resulted in the decision by Ideal's diminutive president, Lionel Weintraub, to abandon board games. I remember his high-pitched voice saying to me, "Phil, we were making good money on dolls, toys, and hobby kits. But we were arguing all the time about games. It was chaos. I hated it. I finally said, 'Why should I bang my head against the wall and waste more of our money every year? Parker Brothers and Milton Bradley own the board game business. Let's drop it.'"

Haunted House was created by the nation's most powerful "house of toy invention"—Marvin Glass and Associates of Chicago. Marvin Glass himself was a post-World War II marvel—a strong-minded man who kept odd hours, hardly slept, and drove others (especially his many wives and business partners) nuts. His lucrative income from toy royalties enabled him to build a powerful organization, which included seven very talented associate partners and teams of model-makers, designers, and graphic artists (and also made it easy for him to attract glamorous women, despite his self-acknowledged homely looks).

But Marvin Glass was not an inventor. Rather, he was a brilliant salesman of inventions and a scavenger par excellence who found new ideas for toys in the most unlikely places. By pure chance, in 1962, he spotted a Rube Goldberg cartoon while thumbing through a newspaper while he was berating Burt Meyer, one of his trusted associates, to invent more toy ideas. Marvin showed the cartoon to Burt and suggested he come up with a product based on the contraption pictured in the cartoon. Today, many would ask, "Who is Rube Goldberg?" Back then, he was a household name.

Reuben "Rube" Goldberg was a cartoonist, sculptor, and engineer who won a Pulitzer Prize in 1948 for his political cartooning. However, he was best known for his illustrations of ridiculously complicated machines that performed simple tasks (like loosening an egg from its shell—beginning with a caged bird eating birdseed that triggered a series of levers until a small hammer tapped the suspended egg—or building a "better" mousetrap that lured a mouse, captured it, put it inside a rocket, and then blasted off to the moon to get rid of it). He even marketed a card game, "Foolish Questions," and self-promoted it.

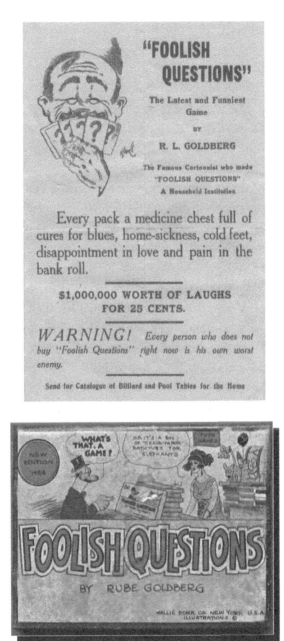

Though Glass and Meyer were not looking at Goldberg's mousetrap contraption that day, they quickly decided that a comical mousetrap would be the contraption they should make. They knew that Ideal Toy, one of their firm's biggest clients, had a successful plastic hobby kit line. So initially, it made sense to develop this mousetrap as a put-together plastic kit, complete with a steel ball bearing that would cause each "gimmick" along the way to swing into action, until a trap (whatever it might be) snapped "shut."

Meyer gave the assignment to Gordon Barlow, one of the firm's designers. Barlow was a "game guy." He didn't think much of it, but his fertile mind came up with an idea: Why not attach the mousetrap thingamajig to a game board?

The original 1963 Mouse Trap® Game by Ideal Toy Corp. Typical retail price: $3.97

Marvin Glass

The device would be assembled as the game progressed. When finished, a bucket would tip a ball that would set off a series of silly gadgets until a cage on a pole ratcheted down over a mouse of one of the players. Last mouse left won the game. *Voila!* Plastics had joined cardboard to make an "action" board game. The play was inane, but it was *fun*.

Lionel Weintraub was the son-in-law of one of Ideal's founders; he had trained as a schoolteacher. He was pressured to take over the firm after tragedy claimed its president in the early 1950s. In time, he developed a gifted knack for picking hit toys.

Photo taken by Phil Orbanes in the Strong Museum

The Gnome is back in time, watching as the Mouse Trap prototype is presented to Weintraub. He reports, "Lionel is not buying. He shakes his head and tells the Glass folks, 'We're not in the game business anymore. This is a game, and an expensive one at that. We failed at board games.' Burt Meyer is undeterred. 'You failed with traditional board games. This one is different. This one *will* put you in the game business.'"

I can picture Lionel Weintraub pursing his lips and squinting, as he was wont to do whenever someone challenged him.

But this time, the Gnome says, "Weintraub chews on the possibility until a wry smile forms. 'Ok, I'll give it a try.'"

By the time Ideal's Bright Eyes finish with it, Mouse Trap looks and works great. But the Drummers are thwarted by the trade's skepticism, because it has never seen anything like Mouse Trap. The buyers have no reference to judge its sales appeal. In desperation, Weintraub decides to fund an early television ad campaign that summer in one city to see if Mouse Trap has "legs."

The commercial features this very catchy jingle: "Just turn the crank, and snap the plant, and boot the marble right down the chute, now watch it roll and hit the pole, and knock the ball in the rub-a-dub tub, which hits the man into the pan. The trap is set, here comes the net! Mouse Trap, I guarantee, it's the craziest trap you'll ever see."

Summertime is a notoriously bad season for board game sales because people are mainly having fun outdoors. However, in Pittsburg, Mouse Trap captivated TV viewers. Local store shelves emptied. Ideal Toy, encouraged, extended its advertising to more and more cities. Within months, a contagion occurred. Soon, the company could barely keep up with demand.

Ideal would launch more Glass-invented action games the following year. They too sold in "boxcar" numbers. A new category of games was born.

Marvin Glass had a *told-you-so* moment two years later after the plastic action game business had been firmly established, thanks to his firm along with Ideal Toy. He was quoted as saying, "It's knowledgeable people who hold back progress in the toy industry. They have all the answers and their answers are [consistently] wrong."

Two years after this remark, the word "plastics" was memorialized in the movie *The Graduate*. It's still the Gnome's favorite movie. He loves to reenact the scene where a family friend played by Buck Henry corners young Dustin Hoffman. His impersonation of "Mister McGuire's" voice is uncanny. "Ben, I just wanna to say one word to you. Just one word.... Are you listening? Plastics. There's a great future in plastics. Think about it."

After Mouse Trap, the race was on among the major game manufacturers for the next great plastic action game. Most of these would be created by Marvin Glass and Associates (and ex-Glass designers who left for greener pastures). In the warm glow of Mouse Trap's success, they came up with more hybrid cardboard/plastic games. Then Ideal marketed two all-plastic blockbusters—Kerplunk and Battling Tops—and cut the "umbilical chord." From then on, most action games were made entirely of plastic, aside from some ancillary parts like ball bearings. Eventually, electronic components would also be included. (That's another story.)

The Gnome comes around and exhales. "It was obvious to me that nobody in this room knew what they had. I suspect Weintraub agreed to take a chance on Mouse Trap to stay in the good graces of the Marvin Glass Company—and perhaps to keep the game away from a competitor that might make it a hit. That would have likely devastated him."

"Egg on the face if it went elsewhere and became a big success. I've suffered that kind of mistake."

We make our way back to the sidewalk. I feel the breeze whipping up. We begin our drive back to Massachusetts. "Phil, our expert lives not far from your house. Call your wife. Tell her I'm bringing you home!"

I'm not surprised when the Gnome reveals our next expert. We meet with Rene Soriano at lunch a couple of days later in Essex, Massachusetts. Rene has the air of a kid, despite his advancing years. He once told me, with great sincerity, "To be a game designer, you have to think like an eight-year-old." For decades, he has managed to couple child-like simplicity with deep interest in the world around him. Rene happens to be the creator of the aforementioned Kerplunk and Battling Tops games, plus countless more. His resume extends from the beginning of action games to the present.

But we're not breaking bread with him today to merely reminisce; the Gnome values his wisdom. He asks Rene, "You told me there are four kinds of action games, right?"

"Correct," Rene replies, before munching on a fresh-baked potato chip. "I call them 'Watch it Go,' 'Frantic,' 'Left, Right, Shoot, Shoot,' and my favorite, 'Load Up and Bust.'" He adds, "Of course, my Kerplunk game is the inverse. It's 'Unload and Bust.'"

"You pull the jack straws out of the clear cylinder, one by one. Marbles are resting on them. Soon, you pull out a stick and some marbles drop to the tray on the bottom. Eventually, they all fall. Whoever gets the most marbles loses."

The Games Gnome observes, "Therefore, in load-up-and-bust games you keep adding stuff or pressing a lever until something gives way."

"Very good," Rene replies like a professor, pleased with his student. "A balloon bursts, pieces fly into the air, or a whip cream pie hits you in the face."

The Gnome says, "Yum." The waiter has arrived with our meals.

When we finish eating, it's down to business. "How would you characterize Mouse Trap?" I ask.

"Mouse Trap is a Watch-It-Go game once you finish building it. You tip the bucket and the little ball bearing sets it off. You watch the mechanism do its thing until the cage rattles down and traps your poor mouse. Simple, but very clever."

"So, Rene," the Gnome says, "You have seen the action game business unfold from its inception. I have told you about my theory of chaos, chance, wisdom, and immortality. Mouse Trap surely fulfills three of these. But is there wisdom to be learned from it?"

"Sure. Simple lessons. For example, you have to build things right if they are to work reliably. How many times have kids rushed to put together the Mouse Trap device and been disappointed when it doesn't do what is intended? Mouse Trap teaches you need to take your time and not skip vital steps."

"How about another?" I ask.

"What about Newton and his apple?" Rene replies. "Two of that man's famous laws of motion are demonstrated by Mouse Trap. Now, it may seem obvious to us adults that a body at rest wants to stay at rest, but…"

"Meaning: I do not want to move, unless you push me," the Gnome interjects.

"Right. You need a kick in the butt. That's the first law. Newton's third law says: for every action there is an equal and opposite reaction."

"Every push pushes back," I offer.

"Yes indeed. And here's my main point: It's much easier to teach kids physics when you can demonstrate these and other laws. Mouse Trap makes for great lab equipment."

"Got more?"

"I do. If you go too far, everything could come crashing down and all your hard work might be for naught. And one more: All things must end. It's fun to build the mechanism and move along the path, but eventually, you're a goner. This fact teaches one other thing about reaching for a goal in life. It may seem arduous to get there, but when you do and you look back on the journey, you realize that was the best part."

On this cheery note, we order dessert.

Chapter Thirteen

INTO OTHER REALMS

When the doorbell rings three days later, Anna doesn't mutter the proverbial, "I wonder who that could be?" She *knows.*

The Gnome is standing there, grinning; he hands her a small bouquet. "Trade you these for your husband," he says.

I make coffee and arrange a tray with cookies while Anna humors him at the dining room table. I listen from the kitchen and hear the enthusiasm in his voice. "Anna, so far Phil and I have examined games that one would probably call 'mainstream' played by families, casual players, perhaps aficionados. But now, I'm going to zero in on two games that cater to a more, shall we say, unique audience. To some, these games even fit into a category named 'Cult.'"

As the mother of two sons who embraced such games as teens and young adults, Anna says, "I can guess their names. Dungeons & Dragons® and Magic: The Gathering®."

"Usually just called 'D&D' and 'Magic.' Both have joined the ranks of immortal games. And both are *so* unique!"

I set down the tray and ask the Gnome, "Is there a connection between the two?"

He replies emphatically. "Both were games that changed the way we played. One begat the other. Richard Channing Garfield, the inventor of Magic, says that it was his youthful love for Dungeons & Dragons that inspired him to create Magic. He also conceived Magic card decks as customizable to make for an endless game, just like D&D."

"Are you going to take me places so you can witness their creation?"

"No, I think we'll stay here and munch while I talk. Both games are recent; you know their beginnings. I know them."

"Let's take them one at a time," I suggest. "The era when Dungeon & Dragons hit the gaming world was a time of turmoil."

"Unsettled conditions seek relief. For many of us, Dungeons & Dragons provided a timely escape. D&D emerged from the transformative 1960s. The Cold War, the Vietnam conflict, and their repercussions were assaulting us daily. It was the era of counter-culture, and no game typified counter-culture more perfectly than D&D. It had its own vocabulary. You and friends could be playing in the same room as your parents and they'd have no idea what you were talking about."

"For example?"

"How about just words in the game beginning with the first two letters: acolyte, acrie, bard, benign, berserk, brigand, and buckler."

Anna laughs, "I remember hearing all of them in our house back then."

"Now, Magic," I say. "After much improvement in the eight-ies, more jolts arrived in the early nineties, and so did another new game, which made an even bigger impact than D&D."

"You are right," the Gnome responds. "The Gulf War was raging in the Middle East and suddenly, in 1991, there was this network called the World Wide Web, which rapidly gained steam and created a new order in communications and information."

"Both games survived their births against great odds. They were different, very different. They did not appeal, at least ini-tially, to the masses. They weren't blasted nationwide in tele-vision commercials. They bubbled up, it seems, carried on the shoulders of more and more enthusiasts."

Dungeons & Dragons allowed players to immerse them-selves in a world of fantasy, similar to what children do with-out even thinking about it. At its inception, the system was unique in its use of a moderator, a "Dungeon Master," who controlled the story as it unfolded. Players represented char-acters with particular strengths determined by the roll of dice. Not just common dice, but multi-sided, up to twenty-sided ones, which when thrown would determine the outcome of confrontations with monsters and villains placed in the game by the Dungeon Master.

Magic: The Gathering also engaged players in a fantasy world, but it is a card game and compels players to buy and collect entire decks of cards—lots of cards—in order to bolster their "game" strengths. They trade these with other players, with the same goal in mind. "Magic" marked the beginning of a new craze. collect ible card games, known by the initials "CCG."

Both games challenged the mental agility of their players. To win against a worthy opponent was as gratifying as beating a master in chess. "Have you talked with many experts about D&D and Magic?" I ask.

The Gnome laughs. "Every serious player I have encountered considers himself an expert. But there are also many *non*-serious players of D&D. In fact, I know entire families who come together to play it." As the Gnome says this, he reaches for his smartphone. "Take Andy Grassie—one of my neighbors in Scotland and a serious Magic fan. We were talking about Magic recently and I recorded what he said." The Gnome fiddles with his phone, until I hear, "…can be very difficult in the beginning. A lot of players later gained entry to the hobby through another card game, 'Pokémon,' though that trading card game is really nothing like Magic. People get hooked on the game and buy more and more cards. Remember, Gnomie, the game is about having the right cards at the right moment and knowing how to play them. Oh, and some of these cards are *very* valuable. I don't mean just in the game, but their real-world financial value. Some people pay a lot of money if they covet a particular Magic card. They keep them in binders within protective sheets."

I slide over to see the Gnome's video; Andy is talking into the camera. He's a tall young man with close-cropped hair and tattoos on his arm that come in and out of view as he gesticulates; at least one appears to be Celtic. In his deep round Scottish brogue, Andy continues, "Dedicated players get quite engrossed in the game, very emotional even. I once watched as a guy got more and more frustrated by his inability to use his Magic cards the way he wanted, and at the end of the game—which he lost terribly and bitterly—he put his hands under the table and lifted the whole thing in the air, flipping it over in sheer frustration. The cards flew every which way. And this was in a public bar where he and others played every Thursday night."

The Gnome skips over parts until he finds the next segment worthy of sharing "…and then they're hooked. You know what else has considerable value to players of Magic? Woman players! There are so few women who play Magic that, as soon as one sits down at the table, the other players get, uh, let's say, energized."

The Gnome tucks his smartphone away and says, "Another neighbor, Hanne Kosinowski in Germany, is a casual player with a keen sense of observation. She told me that one of the differences between the D&D crowd and Magic 'gathering' is that, in Magic, you are literally yourself, whereas in D&D, you take on the identity of a character that becomes your persona every time you play with the same group. You usually have a different character for a different group that is playing another scenario. Your character takes on attributes used during the game. I once heard Hanne explain to a group of newbies that they should not be put off by imagining things such as fire-breathing dragons and 'dismal' dungeons, which some people would consider 'dark.' D&D is nothing more—and nothing less—than a great adventure."

"Just how many experts do you know?" I asked (holding back my curiosity about how he has "neighbors" in different countries; another Gnome mystery).

"Plenty. But we are going to visit only one. Yes, one trip, but not a very long one. We are off to Rochester, New York."

"And who—or what—is there?"

"It is the home of the Strong Museum of Play, of course—the home of almost a half million games and toys. Plus, it is a delightful state-of-the-art museum. Our expert has agreed to meet us there, since he keeps his actual residence a secret. He goes by a code name: Gonrad."

"You mean 'Conrad'?" I suggest.

"No, Gonrad. If you look at the spelling, you will see it is an anagram of 'dragon.'"

"Cool."

"And do not bother to ask. Even I do not know his real name."

Rochester, on the south shore of Lake Ontario, is an impressive but out-of-the-way city that serves, or served, as home for tech firms like Xerox, Kodak, and Bausch + Lomb (now Legacy). The George Eastman Museum is there as well (world's oldest museum dedicated to photography).

As is the Gnome's way, he has already purchased train tickets and, after a four-hour ride on Amtrak, we arrive. "I once got a telegram telling me that Rochester was the birthplace of Western Union," the Gnome remarks as we hail a cab.

You can spend an entire day perusing the public areas of "The Strong"—and even more hours if you are granted access to its burgeoning archives.

"Rochester used to be called the 'Flour City,' because of all the flour mills along the Genesee River," the Gnome informs me during the ride from the station. "Now it is called the 'Flower City' and is home to a famous Lilac Festival. Anna would like it."

We are met at the Strong, located on Manhattan Square Drive, by the head curator for games—Nic Ricketts. Nic and the Gnome are old friends. The Gnome boasts that many of his games are now housed at the Strong, not to mention his impressive collection of American advertising games and premiums. (Gnomes tend to gather; ours now dissipates.)

Dungeons & Dragons got inducted into the National Toy Hall of Fame in 2016, right here at the Strong. The Gnome was on the Selection Committee for this prestigious award.

"What can you tell us about D&D?" I ask Nic—a thoughtful and enthused expert.

"D&D grew out of the miniatures and the wargame movements in the 1970s after there was a rebellion of sorts. Many players were getting tired of pushing cardboard counters that represented vast armies. They wanted something more personal. A revolt occurred. Traumatic at the time, but long overdue. A group of them decided to add *role-playing* to the experience. Two, specifically. Ernest Gary Gygax and Jeff Perrin published rules for a medieval war game they called Chainmail, which was quite different from previous games in the genre because it included fantasy elements. The works of authors like J.R.R. Tolkien and Robert Howard, who wrote the *Conan* series, inspired these folks.

Gary Gygax in 1969 and in later years   *Dave Arneson circa 1970, and in later years*

"Gary belonged to the Castle and Crusade game society, which used miniature figures in its play; then a fellow named David Lance Arneson joined. Dave developed a city and castle game scenario for these miniatures. Chainmail was published at about this time. Dave adopted its rules for a modified campaign and included—drumroll—a dungeon beneath the castle."

"Interesting progression," I comment.

"It gets better. Gygax liked Arneson's game so much that he asked Arneson to take time and write down his rules, which proved convoluted. So Gygax put these instructions in layman's terms and, in doing so, instinctively developed the outline for Dungeons & Dragons."

"Chance meeting, chance combination, a new idea destined to flourish."

"Now comes the Master," the Gnome says in put-on majesty. "The Dungeon Master. A referee, if you will, who narrated the story as it unfolded and, with dice, determined the outcome of battles, other events, and characters' strengths and traits. This marked a *huge* departure from older wargames like those made by Avalon Hill and the 'new order.' The Dungeon Master made D&D unlike anything that had preceded it: he oversaw as each player took on a character, interacted with other characters, and responded to the environment they explored. As a result of to his insights, D&D quickly grew beyond cult status and became immensely popular with a mass of young players."

I note, "Having watched my older son and his friends play, I think there is real benefit in Dungeons & Dragons. It improves socialization skills and helps strengthen friendships. I understand it garnered a lot of support from teachers and scholars, as well as parents."

"You're quite correct," Nic says.

As if on cue, the Strong's Shannon Symonds, another of its curators, enters our room. She is head of The Strong's Women in Games initiative designed to encourage study in the contributions made by women in the development of electronic games. While the Gnome has made arrangements to speak with Shannon later about Magic: The Gathering, her purpose is more immediate. "Your Gonrad appointment is here," she announces. We say our goodbyes to Nic and follow Shannon downstairs into a dimly-lit and windowless storage room in the basement, which, we learn, was chosen so that Gonrad would feel "at home." This tall, youthful man would not raise an eyebrow on the street, but somehow, in this chamber, he looks otherworldly.

"Gonrad, nice to see you again," the Gnome says as we enter the Dungeon-like room. He introduces us and gets right to the point, asking Gonrad to expound his special knowledge of Dungeons & Dragons and Magic: The Gathering.

"I trust you know about Chainmail. What made it different from all the other miniatures rule sets were the 'hero' pieces. Previously, one piece would signify a group of men, like a platoon or squad, or even a battalion. In Chainmail, individual figures represented individual characters, people both powerful and influential. Hero versus hero. At the same time, there was universal resurgence of interest in Tolkien's *Lord of the Rings*, and that influenced game scenarios. Chainmail miniatures were used to reenact key battles in *The Fellowship of the Ring* and *The Hobbit*. In the early days of D&D, miniatures were used, but they were discarded in favor of pure imagination sparked by the prominent role of the Dungeon Master.

"The original D&D consisted of three rules booklets. Men & Magic taught players how to create a hero through imagination and dice rolls. Monsters & Treasure was the first compendium of evil figures that the heroes could fight and the monsters they could earn from victory. Wilderness & Underworld Adventures showed how a player's hero could be a Warrior, a Magic-User, or a Cleric. The names of some of the spoils came directly from Tolkien, such as Nazgul, and Balrogs. But these were phased out, most likely for trademark reasons."

"But lots of paper and cardboard must have been employed given the nature of this revolutionary new game," I note.

"Of course. Players made map boards out of hex paper and graph paper; they could fill a tabletop. Rather than a page or two for instructions, the three rules booklets, combined, numbered over a hundred pages. Strangely, rather than making gamers feel overwhelmed, they clamored for more. As enthusiasm grew, new supplements were added. There were always new monsters to fight and new treasures to find. And the range of player characters grew to include the Thief, Illusionist, Druid, Paladin…many more. Measurable characteristics were added, like Strength, Intelligence, Wisdom, Dexterity, Constitution, and Charisma."

"When did all this really take hold?" I asked.

"By the early 1980s, D&D was a smash hit and began to appear in films and a TV cartoon series. There was great cultural crossover, which verified how popular D&D had become."

"Talk about wisdom, Gonrad," suggests the Gnome.

"Wisdom I can sum up in one word: 'imagination.' Long before the term 'alternate reality' became popular, adults playing D&D could unlock their imaginations, create other worlds, and in doing so, bond with more and more people. D&D brought us 'collective imagination'!"

"Gary Gygax loved fantasy and cherished the imaginative stories he learned as a child. While he did create D&D with Dave Arneson in 1974, the prior year, he co-founded, along with childhood friend Don Kaye, a firm named TSR. It went on to become a very successful company for role-playing and strategy games. He also founded *The Dragon* magazine.

Sadly, this father of role-playing games died in 2008 at age sixty-nine."

"Indeed. Here's a question that must have appeared in one of the Trivial Pursuit editions," I said, trying to lighten the mood after Gonrad's announcement of Gygax's passing. "What does 'TSR' stand for?"

"Too easy," Gonrad and the Gnome shout out at the same time. "Tactical Studies Rules."

The Gnome adds one more. "Maybe only two people in the world know this one: Who came up with the title for the underground D&D adventure, 'Under Illefarn'?"

"Let me guess," I respond, knowing the Gnome all too well. "You did." His grin confirms my hunch.

"Want to talk about Magic: The Gathering?" Gonrad interrupts.

"Yes, you are on a roll. Turn the page. Go forth," replies the Gnome.

"By the early to mid-1990s, D&D settled down but maintained its core following. Then along comes Richard Garfield. He takes the essence of D&D and distills it into cards. Players take on the role of sorcerers battling one another using these cards, which depict magic spells for attack and defense and added enchantments to monsters, including ones you summon and control, in order to attack your opponent. Artifacts add play aspects and land cards provide mana as an energy source to pay for your cards. Voilà, there is no longer any need for a 'Dungeon Master' or referee. Players confront one another directly. Magic becomes the next big thing."

Richard Garfield, younger and older

"Talk more about the cards," I interrupt. "Did everyone have the same access? And how many could you use?"

"Each player customizes a deck that, in the official rules, must contain no less than sixty cards. Most players buy booster packs of cards in hopes of finding the rare and 'mythic rare' powerful ones."

"You can spend a small fortune," the Gnome advises.

"Yes, there's a very commercial aspect to this hobby. There were hundreds of cards from the get-go; now nearly twenty thousand different Magic cards. That means each player has a chance to create a mix that, potentially, no one else has ever put together. Magic has created a collecting mania. People put mint cards into plastic sleeves to protect and organize them, while playing with duplicates."

"Ah, that is what my friend was talking about. So you can play with as many cards as you want?"

"Yes, but the more cards in your deck, the less predictable it is. You start with seven cards in hand and draw one, sometimes more, per turn. Deck creation is a science and an art, with considerable mathematic consideration. You must take into account your opponent's psychology when building a deck to duel this person."

"The rarest card," the Gnome tells us, "is the 'Proposal' card that Richard Garfield made especially to include in a deck, acting as a proposal of marriage to his girlfriend Lily Wu. 'If the proposal is accepted, both players win.' The card came up in their fourth game—and Richard and Lily married."

Before we leave, I ask Gonrad why he keeps both his name and where he lives a secret. "That's also a secret," he replies.

Shannon takes us back to the museum's main floor. An avid Magic player, she considers it her favorite pastime. "I'm not sure how much I can add to what Gonrad already told you. But a company named Wizards of the Coast, back in 1993, released Magic. Richard Garfield was granted the patent on trading card games, which became a multi-billion dollar global industry. There are sixty-five thousand registered tournament players and more than twelve million players in all.

"Magic requires a lot of strategy, but there's also a certain amount of luck. When your life points reach zero, you're done. It's an easy game to learn but difficult to master. Successfully completing a strenuous game can be extremely rewarding."

"There are also electronic iterations of the game," I mention.

"That's right. The first was in 1997. They feature virtual cards." Shannon adds one more fact. "Wizards of the Coast purchased D&D and then Hasbro purchased Wizards. So Hasbro owns this world, so to speak."

"Does the Strong own any special D&D or Magic documents?" I ask.

"We now have two hand-typed volumes called the Dalluhn Manuscript after its previous owner. It was used either as an early prototype or for playtesting and was most likely written by Gygax and Arneson."

We offer our thanks, make our farewell, and are back on Manhattan Square Drive. "And now?" I inquire.

"Phil, we're going to see the former mayor of Fairport, New York, Clark King, who hosts his own weekly Eurogames group. He wants to meet us at Rochester's most famous game store—Just Games. Last year, it carried the limited-edition book, *Dungeons & Dragons Art and Arcana*. Then we're going to the Millennium Games store, which hosts Magic game playing six days a week!"

"You mean we're playing D&D or Magic, tonight?!" I say incredulously.

"No, even better. Later, Clark will escort us to a performance at one of the oldest murder mystery dinner theaters in the country, The Mystery Game. While there is no role-playing for us, it is *live*. Audience members act and speak out. You don't know if the strangers sitting at your table are other guests or real actors. No costumes. A real-time whodunit."

I think back to our beginning with Anthony Pratt and the acting out of "Murder." Seems we've come full circle. What better way than to end a complete day of fantasy game immersion than to enjoy a special evening of reverie and suspense?

CHAPTER FOURTEEN

IS ANYTHING TRULY TRIVIAL?

Once again, the Gnome and I are at Boston's Logan International Airport, waiting for a plane. The weather is iffy; there is no aircraft at our gate, but the status board says it will depart on time. I find myself thinking: They always say that on the board, *until the last minute.*

"Phil," the Gnome says, using an enticing tone that tells me he is about to pop a question I shouldn't be able to answer, "What game was invented by a photo editor and a newspaper sports journalist?"

I tell the Gnome I would appreciate a little more information.

"It was called by *TIME* magazine 'the biggest phenomenon in game history.'"

"Well, you first asked me a trivia question, and then you used the word 'phenomenon.' Put them together, and you must be talking about Trivial Pursuit."

The Gnome's surprise confirms my answer. "Did not think you would get that one. Well, can you guess why we are off to Montreal?"

"That's where it all began?"

"Oh, look," the Gnome is pointing to the board above the ticket agent. "Fight delayed, twenty minutes."

Still no plane is at the gate. Time ticks.

A few hours later, we belatedly exit a taxi in front of a Montreal apartment. "Let's go inside," the Gnome commands. "But before we do, I need to ask you to be patient with me. I have used my rearview mirror a lot in a very short period of time. My mental battery is a bit low, I can sense it."

"What is your goal here?"

"This is a very important place. I need to concentrate and see it as it was forty years ago."

As we look toward the nondescript building, the Gnome tells me that, back then, it housed the apartment of Scott Abbott, one of the two inventors of Trivial Pursuit. In the 1970s, Scott worked as a sports journalist for *The Canadian Press*. He was assigned to cover the 1976 Summer Olympics in Montreal—the first Olympic Games held in Canada. There, he met photojournalist Chris Haney, who was also working the event. They connected; a friendship grew. But Haney, short on cash, had to move away—to Spain of all places—and take up residence in his mother's home. Poverty had brought about chaos in Chris Haney's life. Nevertheless, he married his girlfriend Sarah Crandall in 1977 and they had a child fourteen months later, placing an even further burden on Haney's meager finances.

Haney was finally able to return to Montreal two years later in 1979, thanks to a new job as a photo editor with

The Gazette. The Abbot-Haney friendship was back on high because, still in need, Chris, his wife, and baby John, moved in with Scott Abbott!

Chance, fueled by economics, had set the scene.

The Gnome has, at last, entered his zone. "I am inside their place," he reports, "watching Chris and Scott at the table where they are about to start a game of *Scrabble.* Funny how this game fits into so many stories. Chris realizes there are tiles missing. 'We're six short of a hundred.' The situation is remedied after Chris and Sarah run out to buy a new set. 'I've spent enough money on Scrabble over the years,' he complains upon their return, 'we should just invent our own game. Seems there's money to be made in the game business.' Much like Alfred Butts, who carefully deduced the need for a good crossword game, Scott suggested the team develop a trivia game, because no good ones had yet been marketed. Chris was all in."

Chris Haney and Scott Abbott

I broke in, "Marketing Minds, Hats, and even Bright Eyes do not constrict novice inventors; their creative process is unfettered. And so, Haney and Abbott sketched out a proto-type in less than an hour. It looked like nothing anyone had sketched before.

There was a gameboard, yes, but it was neither a perimeter track board, nor a grid. It looked like a circular ship's wheel, with six 'spokes.' Haney rummaged through other games he owned to come up with plastic playing pieces and some dice. The two composed lists of trivia questions after settling on six categories: arts and literature, entertainment, geography, history, science and nature, sports and leisure."

The idea of their game was to roll and move around the outer "wheel," landing on spaces corresponding to the six categories. A trivia card would be drawn and the appropriate question asked. A correct answer scored for that category and earned a free turn. Once a player had scored in all six categories, he or she would race down one of the" "spokes" to the center space and answer one more trivia question, as selected by the opponent. Whoever did so correctly first would win the game. Pretty simple!

"And by the end of the evening, the two men had come up with what would become not only a great trivia game, but also one of the all-time great game success stories in history. They initially named their creation *Trivia Pursuit*. But Sarah Haney thought Trivial Pursuit® sounded better. They quickly agreed."

"So, did they produce their trivia game themselves? If so, how did they finance such a venture?"

"They did produce Trivial Pursuit themselves, and did so very cleverly. It took two years, but they got thirty or so friends and family members to invest about forty thousand dollars. They then made enough copies of Trivial Pursuit to sell into selected retail shops. Let's zoom five years ahead. The day had arrived when they could hand out envelopes to each investor. Inside was a fifty thousand–dollar dividend check for every five shares each had bought."

"If you know all this 'trivia,' then you must know where the Horn Abbot name came from."

"How could I not?" the Gnome answered, in his usual playful style. "'Abbot' was a shortened version of Scott Abbott's name, and 'Horn'—actually 'The Horn'—was Chris Haney's nickname. To help raise the money and organize the firm, Chris and Scott enticed John Haney, Chris' brother, and their attorney friend, Ed Werner, to join them in forming Horn Abbot Ltd., which officially registered in 1980."

"So Horn Abbot, that is to say, Chris Haney and Scott Abbott, and the other two, made millions from their idea. Right?"

"Absolutely. And so did others. For example, Michael Wurstlin, an eighteen-year-old unemployed graphic designer. He was offered a thousand dollars to design the graphics for the project. With almost no budget, Wurstlin used lots of clip art from art books and designed the question cards and a logo. Ultimately, he accepted five shares instead of the thousand dollars, which eventually brought him such an abundance of capital he started a marketing enterprise in his own name.

"Yet, the game was initially a 'loss-leader,' costing five times more to make than they got from wholesaling it to retailers, who insisted they could never sell it if the retail price exceeded twenty dollars. But Horn Abbott was determined to get the game out there. Eleven hundred copies were released in Canada at the end of 1981."

"This was not a great time to launch a new board game," I realize. "Video games and handheld electronic games were all the rage. I was caught up in this storm both at Parker Brothers and previously at Ideal Toy. Games like Simon—the memory-repeating musical note game by Milton Bradley (another Glass idea)—sold over two million units in 1979. And Parker's Merlin was accorded "Game of the Year" in 1980. Meanwhile, the Atari video game console was fueling sales of game cartridges (by many makers) to such an extent that, if you stacked them on their sides like dominoes, in one year, they'd form a line from Chicago to Paris."

"Precisely," responds the Gnome. "So when Horn Abbot took Trivial Pursuit to the Canadian and New York Toy Fairs in 1982, at the height of the video game craze, the buyers held their collective noses. The common retort was: 'Who the hell will pay thirty dollars for a box of cards, especially when the cards got "used up" in play?'"

I know how brutal the trade can be when pronouncing a death "sentence" for a new game. "The Horn Abbot team must have felt bruised and defeated after these fairs."

"Well, yes. Chris Haney was effectively bankrupt."

"But something worked, right?"

"Fate had another outcome in its fickle mind. What happened reminds me of James Brunot and Scrabble. One day, only a trickle of orders and thought of closing up shop. The next, demand exceeds supply. In fact, more money had to be borrowed to make not just a thousand Trivial Pursuit games or even five thousand, but twenty thousand—and this was only for the Canadian market."

The Gnome continues. "It may not be readily apparent, but it is one thing to get orders for twenty thousand games, it is another to smoothly and quickly supply these goods. Setbacks appeared right away. For example, the only company that could produce the demanded quality card stock could not increase Trivial Pursuit production because they were obligated to supply much of Canada's paperboard packaging. Also, the game's plastic pieces were contracted to a Wisconsin company that had only four full-time employees. The firm owned but three mold presses. The presses couldn't keep up with demand because there's a limit to how many times a molding press can open and close per minute when making plastic parts. A year later, this company had eight presses in operation and gainfully employed at least one hundred twenty Make-Its."

I make an observation. "The Marketing Minds would tell me that ten times as many copies of a game can be sold in the United States as in the Canadian Provinces, based on relative population and interest in game playing."

"Abbott and Haney also knew this and suspected that TP could sell at least two hundred thousand copies in the States. So they went hunting for a game company to license it to."

I feel a wry smile forming. "Naturally, Milton Bradley and Parker Brothers reject the game, saying it costs too much and, besides, the Big Wind in the marketplace has a new name: VIDEO GAMES. There's barely a breeze to flutter the sails of the old ship named Board Games."

"The cardboard game is dead, long live the new whiz-bang game."

"Except the new game didn't thrive much longer. Sales of handheld electronic games and vide cartridges began to falter in 1983. And what's waiting in the wings to pick up the slack?"

"Trivial Pursuit!" The Gnome almost chortles as he says its name. "And which firm earns the cornucopia of orders? Selchow & Righter, the makers of Scrabble and Parcheesi." By now, the firm had not only outgrown its cramped Brooklyn factory, but also the Bay Shore, Long Island plant where some twenty million Scrabble sets had been made. Its current facility in Holbrook, Long Island is really big. Management frets about unused production capacity, so it becomes determined to make TP a hit in the States. The Gnome explains how. "Selchow sends copies of TP to all the celebrities named on the cards in the game, realizing they'd talk it up, much like Prince Oby's celebrities who broadcasted the appeal of backgammon. Word began to spread, rapidly. *Time* magazine featured the game. It became hip to reference TP in print or on TV, much like the Monopoly game back in the mid-1930s."

"So, your theory applies once more…"

The Gnome interrupts. "Except vultures descended, in the form of lawsuits."

"Lawsuits? But Haney and Abbott didn't borrow from another game. Gnomie, I can tell you that the Baby Boomers—our generation—had been keen on trivia contests for many years. I used to play a made-up game called 'Remember When' while in college. We had relatively pleasant childhoods. We were also the first TV generation. We enjoyed looking back as we became adults. Trivia was in our genes. But, and this is important, there was no viable commercial predecessor to Trivial Pursuit. How could Horn Abbot be sued?"

"The suits were not over the game's design or its play, they focused on the trivia questions it contained."

"I see."

"One suit came from the publisher of a trivia encyclopedia series, including the 1979 edition of *The Complete Unabridged Super Trivia Encyclopedia*. The author, Fred. L. Worth, always threw in one or more fake answers to see if anybody was copying his material. When he read a Trivial Pursuit question and answer about the first name of the TV character Columbo being 'Philip,' he knew it had been taken from one of his books. Ultimately, the judge dismissed the three hundred million-dollar suit, saying that the two products were significantly different. Basically, Worth had no 'ownership' of that incorrect trivia."

"Three hundred million dollars? Listen, I know a lot about games and their sales over time, but three hundred million is surreal. Of course, the numbers surrounding Trivial Pursuit dwarfed anything prior in history."

"While this mess was being resolved in 1984, more than twenty million TP sets were sold, recording sales in the neighborhood of eight hundred million dollars for Selchow. Over the next two decades, an additional sixty-eight million sets were purchased—including Trivial Pursuit games printed in more than fifteen languages and selling in more than twenty-five countries."

I add, "The 1984 volume is an all-time record for a board game. Monopoly is still the biggest-selling board game over time, but its best year's sales were a fraction of this bonanza."

"Naturally, TP's success engendered loads of competition. And, for a while, most of these 'me-too' games sold well."

"Bob Reiss's firm quickly published the successful TV Guide Trivia Game; Parker offered the People Magazine Trivia Game and Bradley marketed Ripley's Believe It or Not."

"I was responsible for that one. I'll tell you my story some day," says the Gnome.

"Trivia games became an enduring category of board games. And later came online versions."

"I don't need to tell you about all the specialty editions from a 'Junior Edition' to sports, to baby boomer, to various decades; over two hundred twenty editions in all! The estimated income from worldwide sales of Trivial Pursuit and its plethora of editions is said to be well in excess of one billion dollars."

The Games Gnome tells me, "I know another interesting fact, trivial as it may be. The original game was known as the 'Genus Edition,' as in 'genus' and 'species,' but many mistakenly called it the 'Genius' Edition."

"Right. Say, how do you remember all this stuff?"

"*You* look things up on a computer or in a library, Phil. *I* have my facts on permanent file in my brain, my memory."

"Nice gift."

"And there is more fascinating trivia," the Gnome continues, without a hitch. "Selchow & Righter, the same company that sold Scrabble, licensed Trivial Pursuit from Horn Abbot in 1982, and then, four years later—in a surprise move no one saw coming—Selchow & Righter's owner, Richard Selchow, sold the hundred-and-nineteen-year-old company—the oldest family-owned company in the U.S—to a competitor named Coleco (formerly the "Connecticut Leather Company").

"Coleco, made rich by its recent launch of Cabbage Patch Dolls, was now the owner of three of the games included in our study: Scrabble, Parcheesi, and Trivial Pursuit. But Coleco stumbled. Its prior success with a video game console named ColecoVision compelled it to rush an ambitious home computer, named Adam, into this volatile market. Adam never worked. It was DOA. A travesty."

"Must have eaten a poisoned apple," I joked with humor that sounded more like the Gnome's than my own.

"Its demise had colossal implications." The Gnome shakes his head for emphasis as he laments, "Coleco was forced to file for bankruptcy in 1988 and sell off their North American assets."

I pick up the story. "Parker purchased the rights for Trivial Pursuit. Our president, John Moore, was Canadian by birth and proved instrumental in negotiating the deal I contributed to. We rejuvenated TP with an edition named 'The 1980s' because the decade would end just before it appeared on shelf. Then Hasbro purchased Parker's parent company, at bankruptcy, two years later. To this day, it markets the *Trivial Pursuit* brand." I pause a moment in contemplation. "How come *this* game caught on?"

"Partly the timing." The Gnome continues, "And the questions themselves. One thousand cards, with six questions on every card, one for each category. That's six thousand questions! And the questions were more than just trivial. They not only made you try to remember, they make you think.

"Like you hinted, Phil, baby boomers, many of them educated and with a fair amount of leisure time, were ready for a game of their own, which turned out to be a *social* game—a party game, if you will. The thirty-somethings wanted more than just hanging out in a bar or in front of the TV, and here was a game that a large group could play sitting around the gameboard, or in the bar *without* the board. And only one member of the group needed to own a set. In real life, money was, again, a major topic of worry. There had been a recession lasting from 1973 through 1975; some people still had not recovered from it. Then came the energy crisis in 1979, and another full-blown recession in 1981. The U.S. unemployment rate was eleven percent—higher than at any time since the Great Depression. Disposable income nose-dived. Canadians especially suffered, thanks to an inflation rate of more than twelve percent, a situation made worse by the decision of the U.S. to float the dollar's exchange rate, which compelled a devaluation of the Canadian dollar."

"But like Monopoly and the Depression, anyone who wanted TP found the funds to buy a set during this downturn…. Say, what happened with Chris Haney and Scott Abbott?" I ask.

"I will tell you. Chris Haney was twenty-nine years old when he and Scott Abbott teamed up to create Trivial Pursuit. He had dropped out of high school in his senior year, and when later asked about it, said his only regret is not having dropped out earlier. Scott Abbott, on the other hand, has gotten a master's degree in journalism from the University of Tennessee.

"Haney was said to be a compulsive man and, at age fifty-nine, his drinking and other demons led to his illness and death, attributed to heart disease and kidney failure. As for Scott Abbott, he is still going strong, but limits his exposure on social media and in the press, aside from his philanthropic and investing interests. He is active and owns a racing stable, a golf course, and a hockey team."

The Gnome began to fiddle with his belongings, motioning that I should do the same.

"You know the drill, Phil. We have got to hurry to catch another plane. To Chicago this time. Alas, you will have to come back on your own if you want to take in the great sights of Montreal. We can talk about what lies ahead during the flight. Two hours and twenty minutes—which is fifteen minutes quicker than Boston to Chicago, but a lot more expensive. How's that for trivia?"

Once in the air, the Gnome adds, "We are headed to the home of Mike P."

"As in 'p-e-a'?"

"No, 'P' period. Just the letter 'P.' Think of it as 'P' for 'private.' The now-aged Mike P. is someone I have known a long time. He is *more* than aged, actually, he is, like, ancient. But he seems to have gnome-like qualities, so he is handling it well. We share some features, though I am much more the handsome one. We are spry, despite our advancing years. We have a similar sense of sarcasm, sometimes even sardonic humor, and a youthful outlook on life. There is nothing so serious that you can't wring a smile out of it."

"I remember Victor Watson said something quite similar, with that twinkle in his eyes."

"Victor earned his honorary gnome status many times over."

"So Mike P. is gnome-like, and also a man of mystery?"

The Mysterious Mike P.

"As he desires. I talk about him as 'ancient' because his wisdom exceeds the ages. Mike told me that the reason Trivial Pursuit became popular was that it was more than trivial. Meaning and information lurked behind many of the questions. Stuff that made you want to know more and incited you to look things up."

"How did you and Mike P. meet way back when?"

"It was in Israel. We both had assumed different identities." The Gnome's grin suggested there was more to this—or I should say less to this—than he was letting on. "We worked together, keeping our faces hidden and our bodies out of sight."

"Okay, simple question," I interrupted, "what kind of work were you doing?"

"We were puppeteers, working in an educational television series teaching English." He chuckled. "We have stayed in touch for over forty-five years."

With nary a pause, the Gnome filled me in on his personal history with Trivial Pursuit. "Back in the day, I wrote trivia questions for the game after it was purchased by Parker Brothers. I sat in the equivalent of a smoke-filled room—except there was no smoke—with three other Bright Eyes, hashing out the best trivia and trying to outdo each other with our questions and answers."

"Did you like writing trivia?" I was curious because, while I can picture the Gnome pouring over hordes of interesting facts, devouring books and old newspapers—I struggle to imagine him chained to a desk for too long.

"Yes and no. The material itself was fascinating. But eventually everything you did, everything you saw, everything you read, became a piece of trivia. You could not get away from it, could not stop thinking about it. For example, you are having a conversation with a bespectacled woman who was looking over the top of her glasses as she speaks. You stop listening and start thinking, 'Who invented bifocals?'"

"Benjamin Franklin," I blurt out.

"What a know-it-all! Of course, I would expect you to know that since Winning Moves produced the special Know-It-All edition of Trivial Pursuit under license from Hasbro."

"You wrote many of those questions, if I remember, including the one on bifocals."

"My team had to come up with a thousand questions; I made sure I wrote five hundred and one! And that helped Mike and me to stay in touch. He wrote many of these questions and was responsible for the Chicago bonus questions for the Know-It-All Edition."

"Clever idea, tailoring a version for a big city like Chicago."

"'How well do you know your city?' was its teaser." I think of something else. "Was Mike involved otherwise in the game business?"

"Mike helped Barbara, his charming and attractive wife, with ideas for wooden jigsaw puzzles that she designed for kindergarten and preschool children. Trivia time. Mike is the only font of wisdom we will encounter on our journey who is not steeped in games. He was a terrific history teacher for umpteen years. Many of his students have gone into research, politics, and social services. He loved to teach in order to share what he knew. His relentless studies filled him with knowledge and pleasure, which he believed provided an understanding of how the world works, for good and for evil."

"Understanding both the good and the bad makes life more comprehendible," I venture.

As we approach a beautiful condominium in the Village of Deerfield, Illinois, the Gnome remarks, "It has been too long between visits. Here is more trivia. This development, Coromandel, is named for the area in New Zealand where their architect was born."

At the front door, Mike greets the Gnome like a long-lost friend. He warmly greets me as well, as if we've known each other for almost as long. Wife, Barbara, is by his side, and with her first words the brains and beauty of her nature show through. Barbara has been teaching for fifty years and is now *considering* retirement. The Gnome greets her with a big smile and a hug, and comments about how could Mike ever have landed a woman like her. (I suspect he says this every time they meet.)

In the main living area, one is immediately struck by the art that hangs in vivid contrast to the room's white walls, white carpet, and white blinds. Chagall, Picasso, Matisse, and Miró stand out as colorful images that seem to dance before your eyes. Two dark brown sofas add warmth; unique lighting illuminates the contrasting colors; a bookcase topped by photos shows off three grown children and multiple grandchildren.

"Whose work is that?" I ask, pointing to a watercolor of a baby penguin wearing jeweled flip-flops, thinking: Perhaps Picasso? Maybe Chagall?

"Marge Blair. She's a neighbor and good friend."

I ask Mike what wisdom he thought a game like Trivial Pursuit gifts us.

"A democratic society needs people who can think rationally. The pursuit of the trivial—and not so trivial—is one way in which people learn to see and comprehend relationships among other people and things. History is essential to society. Trivial Pursuit provides one effective way to link small pieces in the past to a larger understanding of who we are today. Used properly, this game can be important in developing rational thinking."

"Why do you think the game has endured for so long?"

"Timing, but I imagine you know that as well. The baby boomers grew up respecting the effort needed to acquire knowledge and retain it. That is, before facts and falsehoods became available at the touch of a finger through the Internet."

"And therefore, disposable," I reply. "Board games had traditionally been aimed at the family market. TP is clearly an adult-oriented game."

"Very important, and just right for an aging population that knew the substance of its questions. Trivial Pursuit questions feature information that everybody knows something about, or at least a tantalizing part of the answers. It may be familiar stuff but is often a bit elusive."

"It is an 'on-the-tip-of-my-tongue' kind of thing," the Gnome says.

Mike P. continues. "It's not just trivia; it's history. People derive personal satisfaction from knowing more than they suspect they know, especially when part of a winning team. Trivial Pursuit is, maybe, the best team game in history. This is why the game is played with cards only as often as with a gameboard and pieces. No need to gather around a table when played sans board."

It is getting late and we are all hungry. Chinese is suggested. A vision of Meg and Chinese Checkers flashes inside my head. We go out.

After an evening of great conversation, humor, and a good night's sleep, we make our warm good-byes.

On the way home, the Gnome says, "Knowledge is little more than facts. Wisdom is the ability to understand something you've likely never seen or encountered before because you are capable of making a connection to relevant, or even disparate, experiences in your past."

"Mike P. does that especially well."

"And that's not trivial. *Good* trivia is anything but trivial."

CHAPTER FIFTEEN

THE GERMAN PHENOMENA

"Get ready for your next journey, Phil. It is to a place no one has ever been before."

"Really?"

"Truly."

The Gnome, it turns out, has several abodes in the United States. We're in his Rhode Island place (where the Gnome casts his votes). I happen to notice my chair has seatbelts attached to it. "A very old and comfortable airline seat I picked up at the Brimfield Show flea market," he offers as I fiddle with the belt buckle.

"Where are we off to now?" I ask.

"Not 'we,'" he replies with a wry smile. "You are going on your own! To the island of Catan! So buckle up."

"Catan? Are you thinking of Carcassonne, which is the name of a game and a real town in the south of France? Catan is only a game; the place doesn't exist."

"But it does—at least in the minds of millions of game players. More importantly, Catan, pure and simple, is the most significant new board game in the twenty-first century. It is replete with wisdom and on its way to immortality. And it certainly was born in chaos and…"

"But it is mythical," I protest. "How can you send me to…"

"Phil, listen up. The fact that this place is mythical makes the journey—your journey—far more interesting. I will guide you there, in your own mind."

I hear the Twilight Zone theme dancing in my brain. Do-do-do-do.

But this I "do" know. "The Settlers of Catan®" was first published in 1995 by a German company named Kosmos. "Catan" became so well known that, by 2015, the company decided to change its own name to "Catan." The game's inventor, German author Klaus Teuber—a kindly man with receding hairline—had already made quite a mark. He won Germany's highest honor in 1988 for his game "Barbarossa—the Game of the Year" (Spiel des Jahres). Two years later, he again won for his game *"Adel verpflichtet"* ("By Hook or Crook," aka "Hoity Toity" in the U.S.). The very next year, his *"Drunter und Drüber,"* won Game of the Year as well; it was published in the U.S. as "Wacky Wacky West."

Of course, most notably, Settlers of Catan won in 1995. He was forty-three at the time.

And there is even more significance to Teuber's accomplishments. The burgeoning category of "Eurogames" can trace its origin to 1991 when Avalon Hill published the U.S version of By Hook or Crook. Since then, games created in Europe (mainly Germany) and imported to America have become a mainstay for game players. They offer a bit of complexity coupled with "easy entry." That is, rules that are not complicated and therefore easy for new players to comprehend to grasp the game. Eurogames also have good "repeat play"—which is to say you wanted to play again right away or soon, and often. The category was expanding nicely, thank you, until Settlers of Catan arrived. Then it *exploded*.

The Games Gnome has worked himself into a trance-like state once more. "Okay, Phil. I'm ready to take you away. Hold on and close your eyes." Of course, I am skeptical. Of course, nothing happens...until...wait...I am everywhere, it seems, in this new world. I can see settlements plus men and women working to develop them into cities. The area is divided into plots of land, all hexagonally shaped. There are piles of cut wood in the forest and sheep—lots of 'em—in the pastures. As I float through my dreamscape, I see mines filled with ore extracted by able-bodied miners and bricklayers constructing houses out of bricks. In the distance are fields of grain, blowing in the wind. I touch down. From where I stand, many roads lead to enticing villages and cities, all of which beckon me. A gentle breeze stirs; everything seems quite serene. I hear myself saying, "*The breeze…*"

"Sorry, I'll close the window," the Gnome barks, jarring me out of my dream.

"That was really pleasant," I report, as I clear the remnants and return to the here and now.

"I actually took you into a story inspired by a book. A novel written by Rebecca Gablé. published in Germany in 2003 and translated into English. It is set in 850 A.D. and describes the exploits of a group of Norsemen seeking to discover the mythical island of Catan. The book was the result of Klaus Teuber consulting with the author at a time when he was also considering a Catan novel."

"Teuber and Catan are so well known in Germany, a book has been written about them as well, I hear."

"*Im Zeichen des Sechsecks* is its name, which means 'under the sign of the hexagon.' Peter Gustav Bartschat wrote that one. If you are a Catan player, you will devour its information."

"In such a short time, Catan has become a world unto itself, it seems."

The Gnome agrees. "Unlike Monopoly or Scrabble—whose serious players will become annoyed when new variations appear—Catan is replete with expansions, versions, and accoutrements. Expansions build on basic game play and add something new to play. I have the Glen Grant Whisky edition from 1997 that comes in an oversized tin tube and contains all the playing pieces and a small bottle of whisky as well. Versions are stand-alone games with different play. There were ninety-eight expansions of Catan and seventy-eight versions or editions at my last count, plus more than twenty accessories, including a Catan game table, wooden Viking pieces, pewter pieces, token sets, coasters showing building costs, and a figurine representing the 'robber trio.'"

"I hear this one became a valuable collectible; the limited-run rare robber figures in hard plastic were given away free at special events and were so popular that Klaus Teuber eventually had a larger batch made in tin."

"There is even a Settlers of Catan bus keychain, representing the game's bus that went to cities in Germany to invite people to play."

I've played Catan many times. The original German version was set in a sort of medieval period, while the American edition was altered to depict soldiers in uniforms reminiscent of the Republican troops during the American Revolutionary War. No matter, the games play the same. It goes like this...

After assembling the cardboard frame, hexagonal terrain pieces are placed within it (at random) to create a unique gameboard and then numbered cardboard discs are placed on each one. A "robber" piece begins on the single desert space. Five different resources are produced, depending on the terrain: woods (forests) make lumber (wood); pastures showing sheep make wool; fields, grain; mountains, ore; and hills, bricks (also referred to as clay, the direct translation from the German). Players receive their own set of game pieces consisting of settlements and cities which, during the game, are placed at the corners of hexes, and roads that are placed along the terrain boundaries. Building a settlement, city, or road requires a number of different resources. Two dice govern which hexagon will provide resources to all players with adjacent settlements or cities. (Klaus Teuber says he doesn't like games that have no luck factor. "Luck means the better player won't always win.")

However, a bit of luck is in play, because the Development Card you choose to buy may not fulfill your greatest need at that moment. Each settlement provides a single victory point; each city gives you two. Roads must connect them. In the basic game, ten victory points signals the end of the game. That's pretty much it, really.

"To avoid a trademark hassle, Klaus Teuber decided not to call the game, simply, 'The Settlers.' So he came up with a unique name: The Settlers of Catan. Teuber loves Viking stories. 'They inspired me,' he has said on more than one occasion. In Iceland, 'They need wood; they need houses.' It was also his wish to create a peaceful game with a lot of interaction."

By the end of the 1990s, Klaus Teuber gave up his (not particularly liked) job as a dental technician and began to work full time as a game inventor.

"I understand he considered game inventing to be a very good hobby."

The Gnome chortles. "Hobby? Ha! He has got an empire. In 2002, he incorporated as Catan GmbH, a family business that includes his wife Claudia, the ever-present game tester and keeper of the books; Guido, his eldest son, who lived in the U.S. for a time handling the American distribution and marketing of Catan through Mayfair; and Benjamin—'Benny'—who takes care of the international end of the business. Benny says, 'The beauty of Catan is that, in the end, you still have constructed something. In a way, everybody wins.' Guido loves Catan because, 'The game was born out of a story but it also creates stories.' The only family member not in the firm is the Teuber's daughter, who is an actress."

"Nice to see such a strong family."

"Phil, there is also PlayCatan.com with over eighty thousand active members! You might even wind up playing against Guido or Benny, or Klaus himself—though you won't know it; he plays under a pseudonym."

"Catan is one of the great board games, truly."

"On both sides of the aisle," the gnome adds.

"What do you mean, Gnomie? Republicans and Democrats? Germans and Americans?"

"Neither. I mean serious players and also casual players. Catan bridges that gap. It actually induces causal game players to advance to strategic play."

The Gnome begins gathering his things; we must be ready to embark on the next leg of this adventure. "Sorry. Another long trip. We must go to Germany now," he announces. "You can sleep, I will watch movies."

"Are we going to visit Klaus Teuber?"

"No, I am afraid not. I just heard from Guido." He pulls out his smartphone and shows me part of an email that reads, 'We appreciate hearing from you. Unfortunately, our schedule is full, so we won't be able to take you up on your offer.'"

"So what's in Germany for us, then?"

"Our expert."

"Who is?"

"Sybille Aminzadah. She lives in a small village north of Hanover. Sybille is not only a player, she is a researcher who compiled a broad survey on the differences between German and American Catan players and why they play. We had this discussion at the Essen Spiel event in 2015."

"I used to travel there every October."

"'Essen' in Deutsche also means 'to eat'. And at this—the world's largest game fair—thousands of players *devour* scads of new board games, so to speak. Entire families pay serious money to sit down and play the newest games on the German market, and many compete in the Catan tournament."

"Did you play?"

"No," replies the Gnome. "I was taking loads of photographs of the largest game of Catan ever played."

At "Hannover" Airport (that's how it's spelled here) we are met by a charming woman whose English in tinged only slightly by a German accent. Forty-five minutes later, I am admiring her gardens.

Sybille invites us up to her a second-floor apartment, with its spectacular views of fields and "feathered friends" flying above. Each of her rooms is "pleasantly cluttered," per the Gnome. They are filled with small, interesting artifacts from around the world. Most significantly, her Catan games fill an entire set of shelves.

We sit down for tea and homemade *"Apfelkuchen"*—apple pie. I drink from a Catan mug—which Sybille won at a tournament. "The Gnome tells me you researched how people play Catan in Europe and the US," I say.

"I was curious. I became part of the Catan community and played weekly with my family and game friends. I began to wonder why this game, of all Eurogames, had become so popular."

"Sybille devised a survey, Phil."

"Right, I created a questionnaire and distributed it at game fairs, like Essen Spiel, and also online. I was able to place my survey on the Settlers website, which is siedeln.de."

"How many responses did you get?" I ask her.

"Four thousand six hundred responses from around the world. The results of my survey confirm what I suspected: Catan is so unique and so popular because it is an easy game to learn, but it also has considerable depth. It is energized through its system of trading. Much player interaction. That's very, very well liked. There is tremendous variability in the set-up of the playing area and the use of the variants you play with. All this from a game whose mechanisms are not brand new. Just newly combined."

The Gnome adds, "Variability gives players all over the world the incentive to invent their own scenarios. And they can communicate them through the Internet, or in person."

"Were the survey participants of all ages?" I asked, "And was it an even mix of male and female?"

"Although over one-third of the players in Germany are female, only fifteen percent of American and Canadian players are of my sex. So most survey respondents were male. Eighty percent were between twenty-one and forty years of age."

"How do people learn about Catan?" I asked.

"That was one of my survey questions. Most people heard about the game through word of mouth, and in Germany also from in-store displays and reviews in game magazines. Without such a culture, far fewer in America saw the game in stores or read reviews. But this was in 2004. Things have changed a lot since. In 2008, the tipping point was reached in the U.S and sales surged, according to Mayfair Games."

"That's when the crowd really developed," the Gnome adds. "And curiously, as Sybille can tell you, Americans were buying and playing Catan mainly to have fun."

"We Germans tend to focus on the strategy of the game," Sybille notes. Our players seek first to learn what to do and not do to win the game. For example, Guido Teuber says to 'build cities as early as possible in the game.' Klaus Teuber advises, 'Never build the longest road at the beginning. It could delay your building settlements.'"

I offer a few observations. "In the U.S., entertainment rules. Catan is a favorite of one of the characters on the TV series 'Parks and Recreation.' It's also been featured in episodes of shows like 'The Big Bang Theory' and 'Madam Secretary.'"

The Gnome continues, "I hear that film producer Gail Katz of 'Air Force One' and 'The Perfect Storm' fame purchased the film and television rights for the game, and an upcoming movie has been announced. The story will be by Klaus Teuber and Blaise Hemingway."

"'Techies love the game as well," Sybille adds, "playing it during corporate retreats. Mozilla's former CEO John Lilly told *The Wall Street Journal* that the game is popular with the I.T. community because it 'most closely approximates entrepreneurial strategy.'"

"'There's even a Star Trek edition," the gnome says excitedly. "Instead of accumulating wood, grain, and wool, you collect oxygen, water, and the substance 'dilithium'; you do not construct roads, you create enterprises. The game includes cards representing characters from the original series, each with a special ability to be used during the game."

We begin to talk about the game's imparted wisdom. *The Washington Post* called Catan the "board game of our time." Columnist Blake Eskin believes that Settlers of Catan had taken hold because it exemplifies modern life, where we are presented with limited resources and living in a time of intertwined global economies. Others have described Catan's success as a geek game gone mainstream.

Sybille adds, "Many see the game as thematically correct, fictional but not science fiction, competitive but not combative, and one that fosters the imagination rather than imposing rigid scenarios."

"And where was the chaos that prompted the game's initial creation?" I ask the Gnome.

"First and foremost, the chaos that spawned Catan began right after the Second World War. Anything to do with militarism in Germany was either banned or frowned upon. By now, several generations of Germans have grown up with this philosophy inculcated. This really affects German games, because, throughout history, most great games were based on conflict and competition. The easiest—some say the most natural—way to determine a winner in a game is for one to prevail while all others fall by the wayside or fail to reach the finish line."

In a flash, I think of chess and backgammon and Risk and Monopoly.

"So Teuber was compelled to invent a game that stressed cooperation and trading, not conquest," the Gnome observes. "And somehow make it exciting. No small task. Oh, and then there was the economy, back in the U.S."

I think quickly. "Of course. Both on a national level and in the game industry itself."

"The game premiered in the U.S., during the mid-nineties, after a decade of consolidation, by Hasbro, of most American game companies, including Milton Bradley in 1984 and Parker Brothers in 1991. And the likes of Selchow & Righter, Coleco, Ideal, Lakeside, and others. Then there was the economy. It had suffered from rampant inflation for so long most thought it couldn't be contained. But the Federal Reserve knew it had to stop it. It took extreme action. Interest rates were raised to astronomical levels and, inevitably, a recession set in while the 'medicine' was applied."

I interject, "As we've seen, leisure time activities, like movies and games, often thrive during downturns like that one."

"Correct," Sybille says. "Many think the public was primed for a new game to divert its worries—much like Trivial Pursuit a decade earlier. Even though Catan was invented in Germany, it had no competition; no new homegrown game had burst forth."

"And what about chance?" I ask. "Was Catan ever in danger of not making it?"

The Gnome becomes animated. "Phil, you have been to the International Toy Fair in Nuremberg, Germany. Hundreds, maybe thousands, of new games are introduced there each January. Most of these new games are never heard of again. Catan was only a needle in the haystack when it premiered. It attracted just enough attention to get reviewed and nominated for Game of the Year. Somehow, it prevailed over stiff competition and won the big prize. I have seen entire companies crash and burn because their new game did not win Game of the Year. Take it from me, the difference in sales between the winner and the other nominees is like twenty or fifty to one. Imagine if Catan had not come in first!"

"You sold me. Now, is there more wisdom to talk about?"

"Tell Phil," Sybille says, nudging the Gnome, who needs no encouragement.

"Yes. Yes. This trading game teaches: you can't have everything. So you need to accept the need to give up something in exchange for something else you *really* need. Catan, given its core principles, instills the merit of cooperation over conflict.

Not every moment in life needs to be spent bucking heads or trying to outwit an aggressive foe."

Sybille notes, "Working together for mutual benefit gains far more enduring results, and without unintended consequences."

The time with our charming host has come to an end. I look out her window, and for a moment, imagine her fields are hexagonal in shape, populated by traders exchanging wood for sheep...that life is good.

We will soon embark on a very long flight. But the Gnome has comforted me: this one is to be our last.

CHAPTER SIXTEEN

LIFE STILL GOES ON

ig Bob is a friend—and "affable." Bob would be yours too if I could introduce you. He is waiting for me (the Gnome will arrive later) at a shaded picnic table, here in East Longmeadow, Massachusetts, not far from the main entrance of the "Big House."

Bob is a rather imposing fellow whose resonant voice would be the envy of any radio announcer. He is made from proverbial salt of the earth (prompting some to call him, "one big salty dog"). Of course, "Big Bob" is his pseudonym, like some other names you've met in prior chapters that are, by choice, alter egos. *(Silly me; I thought "egos" wanted to become famous!).*

Big Bob and his father (the "Big Bob" before him) once knew everything about the "Big House" because they worked inside it for so long. This Big House is not a prison like Sing Sing—the correctional facility thirty miles north of New York City where Wall Street Not-So-Good-Doers sometimes gain admission. It's shorthand for the "Big House of Games"—the largest dedicated games factory in North America (and maybe the world).

Bob is sipping Diet Pepsi through a straw; there's a Donut House coffee waiting for me. Employees come and go through the parking lot. Big Bob knows most of them. He waves; he gestures. He says things like "Okay, Frank," and "Ellen. O-kay." Big Bob nuances the word "okay" better than anyone I know. He can use it ten different ways without creating confusion. I am not surprised when he begins by saying, "Okay? It's like this." (Meaning: do you get what I'm about to say? *Pay attention; I know this stuff; I'm not going to waste your time.*) Big Bob doesn't BS. I appreciate that. "Phil, The Game of Life® gave birth to the Big House. Okay, that's a fact."

His blue eyes move in the direction of the Big House; his chary face becomes respectful, reverent. If what he says is true, this building is one hell of an "offspring." It gleams in the sunlight. Its pure white color reminds me of the original Game of Life package whose whiteness stood out in striking contrast to the reds and blues that prevailed in game stores during the 1960s.

The Big House stretches for nearly a quarter mile. Its roof keeps the rain off almost a million square feet of real estate. Chances are, if you own an American board game, it was made inside these four walls.

Bob speaks. "For a hundred years, the game industry was dominated by two companies: Parker Brothers and Milton Bradley. They were the 'Dynamic Duo' in games—just like there was the 'Big Three' domestic auto makers, the 'Five Sisters' petroleum companies, and, in computing, 'IBM and the Seven Dwarfs.' Okay, there were some medium-sized game companies too. But I mean, these were the 'Jokers.' Pressman, Selchow, and Lakeside, and Ideal, and Kohner Brothers and…I can't remember the others. Each of 'em had a hit game or two.

Sometimes, like wild cards, one of the Jokers would trump us. That was okay, it didn't matter. In the end, they disappeared, and Milton Bradley got most of their games. Bradley itself got bought by Hasbro. And Hasbro ended up buying Parker Brothers too. Thereafter, the Big House manufactured seventy-five percent of all the games sold in America. It was great to work here. Even the Games Gnome served time here when we needed him. Okay, you know that, right?"

I do. "The Gnome is making a stop along the way. Rather urgent."

Big Bob reaches into his pocket and produces two snapshots. "I have pictures to show you, Phil."

"The first one shows Milton Bradley's factory in Springfield, Massachusetts, when

The Game of Life was introduced. It was made of bricks. It was old and inefficient. The second photo shows the sleek, steel-and-concrete Big House. Milton Bradley financed it, thanks to the sales of The Game of Life during its first five years."

"Tell me how it happened."

Bob's straw runs dry. He makes a satisfied sound. His story goes something like this.

By the summer of 1959, Milton Bradley was at a cross-roads. Its best sellers were Concentration, based on the popular TV game show, and Rack-o, which included four plastic card racks. However, it hadn't had a new hit board game in years. Parker's board game successes bugged the MB Hats no end. Bradley's even bigger worry was its lack of a new game to feature at the firm's hundredth anniversary celebration the following year.

The Milton Bradley Company began in 1860 when Abe Lincoln was running for president. Milton Bradley—the man—was a printer whose poster of a clean-shaven Abe Lincoln proved to be a huge seller. That is, until Honest Abe went and grew a beard. That became a crisis for Mister Bradley. A friend suggested he try printing a game. After some thought, he came up with the "Checkered Game of Life." For a while, it was the country's best-selling game.

Mister Bradley was very interested in education and, during the next hundred years, his firm would make lots of educational and art-related products.

In July of 1959, hoping to sell an art product to the Milton Bradley Company, a toy inventor on the West Coast named Reuben Klamer flew to Springfield, Massachusetts. The man running "MB" during this era was Jim Shea Senior. Shea nixed the art product but felt sorry for Klamer, who had come so far. As legend has it, he "threw Rueben a bone" by suggesting he come up with a game. "We need something exceptional to highlight at our one-hundredth anniversary next year. We're almost out of time to get it done for Toy Fair next March." (Toy Fair being the industry's premier trade show in America.)

Klamer, acting on impulse, replied, "Can I see your archives? It may help me get some ideas." Shea, desperate as he was, agreed—*No outsider ever got into the firm's basement achieves.* Once inside, Klamer spotted the 1860 Checkered Game of Life and...*eureka*—instantly decided to create a modern version. What could be more perfect to celebrate a centennial than an update of the company's original game?

Reuben Klamer and his associates had designed many hit toys, including one for Ideal named "Gaylord the Walking Dog." Other toys were based on popular TV programs like "The Man From U.N.C.L.E." Many incorporated plastics (Rueben was very plastics-savvy) but he didn't know a game from a gear.

On the flight home, Rueben sketched out his preliminary ideas on a cocktail napkin. First and foremost, he wanted a three-dimensional game. Second, he wanted its track to be winding, like a real highway; he didn't want to use a grid like the original "Checkered" game employed, nor a perimeter track as found in Monopoly. Third, he wanted to come up with a "snazzy" device to determine the moves in the game. No dice.

He wrote down the names of three art firms that could potentially help him design the game, compose its rules, and build a prototype. He very quickly settled on Bill Markham's California Product Development company, because he liked its two graphic designers: Leonard Israel and Grace Chambers. They had done fine work for him in the past, took direction well, and the three also got along well. After reaching a verbal agreement with Markham, Reuben met regularly with Leonard and Grace. The prototype began to take shape. Leonard came up with the design for the game's "big white box" and Grace developed the "3-D" gameboard.

Mel Taft, the head of Research & Development for Milton Bradley (the leader of its 'Bright Eyes') informed Klamer that he had meetings with inventors in Los Angeles, six weeks hence. His trip fixed the deadline to complete a working game. Klamer and Markham's designers met that date.

The Game of Life was unveiled to Mel Taft in a private room at Chasen's—a hip restaurant frequented by movie stars. The final prototype included a big gameboard with elevated roadways (the "highways of life"), plus a plastic spinner that made a pleasant noise when spun. There were little cars that accommodated pegs representing members of a growing family. The game's path began at high school graduation and, if successful, ended with retirement at "Millionaire Acres."

Taft loved its potential, but realized it was more glitter than substance. No problem—he figured that, between Klamer and his Bright Eyes back in Springfield, the game could be perfected to meet a cost goal and play smoothly.

Klamer had another ace up his sleeve. One of his business partners was Art Linkletter, a television star wildly popular with kids and highly respected by parents. Linkletter would endorse the game on his daytime program for an entire year! In return for this promotion bonanza, Milton Bradley would have to modestly increase the royalty paid.

The Game of Life became the highest priority inside the old MB factory and, by Toy Fair 1963, was unveiled inside the firm's New York City showroom. Shipments to stores soon began, and by summertime, the game was selling briskly, thanks to Art Linkletter's weekly endorsement.

There were some detractors—those who felt the game was "much ado about nothing." After all, skill was not essential; luck dominated its outcome. However, the spinner Milton

Bradley ultimately designed became the game's best-loved feature. It was just *so much fun* to spin it.

Big Bob now sums up, okay? "So out of the 'we don't have an anniversary game' crisis, to Klamer getting into our archives and discovering the original Checkered Game of Life, to his idea for a novel 3-D game, to making it in just six weeks, to Mel Taft being in LA to see it then. Well, that's one hell of a run of dice rolls. I mean, what are the odds something like this could ever happen again?"

"The Gnome believes all great games begin in stress and survive by chance," I note.

"The Game of Life has since endured for almost six decades," says the Gnome breathlessly. He has arrived, flush and excited.

"Where've you been?" I ask.

"I have come from a flea market in Brimfield, Massachusetts. I know a dealer there. Actually, I know all the dealers, but that is not important. What is important, is this…" He removes from his bag a pristine copy of The Beatles "Flip Your Wig" game. He proudly announces, "It was made *right here*, inside the Big House in 1964."

There they are, the Fab Four—John, Paul, George, and Ringo—on the cover of their "own" game. "That's great," I say, "but what does this have to do with the price of cheese?"

He glares at me. "Phil, we're talking wisdom here. Each of the Beatles knew that life was like a game."

The Gnome elaborates. "John Lennon spoke of playing the game 'Existence' in 'Tomorrow Never Knows.' Ringo Starr covered the great Dobie Gray song, 'Drift Away,' and lamented losing the game, day by day. In homage to Carl Jung, George Harrison's 'Any Road,' told us that if we don't know where we're going, we'll get there. And Paul McCartney's pretty nurse suspected her life was a play (game) in 'Penny Lane.' He assured her it was."

"I married a pretty nurse," I say.

"One of your best decisions, in my opinion," replies the Gnome.

Big Bob is also a rocker. He's got an amazing collection of albums from the sixties, seventies, and eighties. (Make an appointment; he'll take you through it.) "Many artists figured out that we're all playing some kind of game. Like Joe South in 'Games People Play' and 'Head Games' by Foreigner and—once again—John Lennon in 'Mind Games.'"

"They all contributed to the body of wisdom," I note. "But what about The Game of Life, Gnomie? If it's a game of luck, does it teach anything useful?"

"Certainly, it does. It teaches kids what it is like to grow into adulthood. What responsibilities they will have to shoulder. The need to think about a comfortable and secure retirement. What other game shows kids the importance of carrying insurance?"

"All true," says Big Bob. "But there's one overriding lesson in the game, if you ask me."

"I am asking," the Gnome retorts.

"O-k-a-y. I'll spell it out. The Game of Life teaches you that, although you may have other interests, like family and hobbies and traveling, if you don't pay attention to your cash flow, you're not going to be able to enjoy 'em." Big Bob stands up, musters his resonance voice and pronounces, "Money is the dominant force in life."

"Money almost took the life out of Life," I hear myself say.

"Come again?" Big Bob asks.

I look for guidance from the Gnome. He nods. "Tell him, Phil." He turns to Big Bob and impersonates radio legend Paul Harvey. "And now the *rest* of the story."

"Bob, I just served as an expert witness in a legal battle over The Game of Life. Despite the game's endurance, it is still quite mortal, it seems. The outcome in court could have killed the game."

Big Bob sits down. "That lawsuit got some publicity when it began a couple of years back. It had something to do with the verbal agreement between Klamer and Markham, right?"

The Gnome opines, "As the maxim goes, 'no good deed goes unpunished.'"

I pick up the story. Because Milton Bradley was in such a rush to get The Game of Life into development and prepare it for manufacturing, it presented Klamer with a contract almost immediately after the prototype arrived in Springfield. Klamer was ecstatic; he had just invented his first game and a deal for it was already on his desk. He quickly signed on the dotted line. He belatedly went off to see Bill Markham to put their deal into writing. It compensated Markham for the salaries of Leonard and Grace and, as promised, granted Markham a share of the royalties—a reward for the quick turnaround and development input by his designers. However, when Reuben arrived at Markham's office, Bill revealed a different side of his character. He decided to capitalize on Klamer's vulnerability. He threatened to undermine Klamer by telling Milton Bradley it couldn't have The Game of Life because it actually belonged to him. Klamer felt cornered and was told to sign a document composed for Markham, which glorified his role in the game's creation. Klamer sighed, and thinking, "What difference will it make?" he signed. But while the two would share the royalties if the game succeeded, Klamer would lose some money if it failed because he agreed to pay Markham for his designers' salaries. *So be it.*

Every game is subject to three kinds of legal protection. Copyright, trademark, and patent. A copyright protects an expression of an idea, but not the idea itself. Authors are entitled to copyright protection. A trademark grants exclusive use of a name in a particular category of commerce, like games. A patent protects an invented "mechanism," like the contraption in the Mouse Trap game. The Game of Life lawsuit concerned only its copyrights. Milton Bradley had properly registered the title "The Game of Life" with the USPTO (United States Patent and Trademark office). It therefore owned this "mark." A trademark endures as long as it is maintained and in use. No mechanical patents had been applied for.

The Game of Life lawsuit concerned ownership of copyrights that pertained to the game board, the package, and the game's rules. Milton Bradley filed them with the Copyright Office in late 1960. Fifty-six years later, we come to the "spanner in the works," as Victor Watson would say. In 1960, a copyright lasted twenty-eight years and could be renewed for a second twenty-eight-year term. Then, it expired. Hello, 2016.

The "old" copyright law had been replaced during the 1970s. Congress passed a new one that granted copyright protection to an author the moment his/her "expression" of an idea was set forth. And copyright protection would now endure for the life of the author plus fifty years. Nevertheless, The Game of Life's original copyrights expired in 2016 in accordance with the operative law at the time of their inception.

Bill Markham died of cancer in 1992, having been a heavy drinker and smoker. His wife had preceded him. In 1991, Markham, the widower, met a woman who swore undying love to him, apparently after he revealed his perpetual royalty income thanks to The Game of Life. In thirty days, they were wed. In thirty more days, he agreed to adopt all of her children from her first marriage. In eighteen months, he was dead.

Markham had never shared a penny of his royalties with his designers, because they were on salary ("special appreciation" was not, apparently, a consideration for him). All of Bill's opulent royalties, following his demise, were paid to his new widow.

In 2016, a law firm encouraged the widow to make the claim that her deceased husband was the sole inventor of The Game of Life. Therefore, she was entitled to *all* the game's royalties—a nice kick in the butt to Reuben Klamer, who by then, was ninety-three years of age.

Lawsuits were filed against Hasbro—owner of Milton Bradley and The Game of Life—plus Klamer, Linkletter, and another business partner. Countersuits followed. A not-so-splendid time was guaranteed for all.

Leonard Israel, Grace Chambers, and Reuben Klamer testified before the judge in late 2017. Despite reconfirming that Bill Markham did not directly design any component of The

Game of Life's prototype, the plaintiffs persisted. In March of the following year, both sides were asked to present their "expert witness." I was asked to help the defense.

"Okay, time out," Big Bob says. "What does an expert witness do? What do you have to know to be an expert, Phil?"

"An expert witness presents facts in his ken to help the judge—and jury, if one is present—decide the case. In order to be a credible expert, you need to be experienced and really know your stuff. And your knowledge has to be applicable to the timetable in the dispute."

The Gnome elaborates for Bob's benefit. "In this lawsuit, the judge would be interested in how the industry operated back in 1960. A lot has changed since then. So Phil's job was to go back in time and demonstrate what he knew to be true then."

Fortunately, I had started inventing and making games as early as age fifteen. Tom Shaw of Avalon Hill generously helped me learn the ropes. He became my mentor. I learned about the Hats, the Bright Eyes, the Make-Its, and the Drummers during the era when The Game of Life was conceived by a Carrier Pigeon named Reuben Klamer.

The Gnome adds, "Big Bob, it can be stressful to serve as an expert witness. I have been one as well. The other side tries its best to discredit you and to limit your testimony. If the case goes to trial, you sit in the witness box, no one to help you, while the opposing Legal Beagles hammer on you. The judge is watching and listening closely. He needs to figure out if he can rely on your facts and opinions, or if you are filled with hot air."

"How did you do when you were on the stand?" Big Bob asks me, a touch of uncertainly in his big voice.

Before I can answer, the Gnome interrupts, as if he is my attorney. "Phil stood up well. He had already served as an expert three times prior."

"True," I say. "But it was still pretty stressful. You have to get it right. I lost a lot of sleep before the trial."

"Is the case decided?" Bob asks.

"Yes, the Court ruled for Klamer/Hasbro, finding that the prototype made by Markham's designers was 'work for hire' and therefore Markham had no copyright to pursue. Consequently, the plaintiffs were without termination rights. So 'Life' goes on as before."

"Well, okay then," says Big Bob before we both notice a faraway look in the Gnome's blue eyes.

"You look, uh, engrossed in thought," I say to the Gnome. "Are you zoning out?"

"No. I'm just thinking back to when I worked in the Big House, some thirty-five years ago."

"How did you wind up here?" Big Bob asks.

"I was an authority on the history of American games. And a serious collector. I went to Bradley to gather information for a book I was writing. The P.R. person who gave me the private tour remarked, 'There's an opening in the development department. Why don't you apply?'

"I was amused at first, but then realized how great it would be to invent games all day I also thought *what a feather that would be in my red cap*. I applied and was hired.

"I became part of a team of Bright Eyes. A cool bunch of crafty cohorts, led by the man who was to become my mentor, John Vernon. John could open a game box and, without looking at the rules, tell you exactly how the game played. Amazing guy."

"What did you gain from your days at Milton Bradley?" Bob asks.

"I learned something profound right away. John advised me, 'Remember, you are inventing games for one person only: the head buyer at Toys-R-Us. If he or she likes your game, it will sell tens of thousands of copies; if not, the game might not even make it to market.'"

Bob asks, "Did you ever mix with the Hats?"

"Yes, when I was working on the Ripley's Believe It or Not! game."

"Tell Bob about Ripley's," I suggest.

The Gnome was most willing to continue. "By then, Parker Brothers had acquired the rights for Trivial Pursuit. The Hats were most anxious to counter. Bradley secured a license to develop a Ripley's Believe It or Not! game, and I was assigned to the task. The Hats kept close tabs on its progress. Basically, it was a bluffing game that employed weird trivia questions from Ripley's. The game turned out to be the company's bestseller that year…but here's a *real* piece of trivia for you…"

"Yes?"

"The licensor for Ripley's was Bob Whiteman. He was the 'B' in Bettye-B Game Company—Bettye being his wife. Remember our discussion about Mouse Trap? In the 1950s, their firm became the first in the industry to produce three-dimensional game boards using vacuum forming."

"Trivia at its finest," I reply.

The Big House beckons us. Should we go in? We are reluctant because Hasbro no longer owns this monument. A company named Cartamundi, out of Belgium, purchased it a few years ago and, under contract, continues to make games for Hasbro and others. True, most of the people working in the Big House worked for Hasbro. Like Big Bob, we know many of them. We could even sign up for a tour. That might be fun—see how the place has changed. But I already know.

I recall that when the Monopoly game was made by my employer, Parker Brothers, more than twenty Make-Its manned its production line. Victor Watson once said of Waddingtons' Monopoly production, "Our workers felt they had job security for life if assigned to its assembly line." I saw the Monopoly line after it came to the Big House and was automated. Three humans, and a bunch of robots, now man it. I like talking to people, not robots. I visualize all the machines inside: the molding presses, the card cutters and collators, the box wrappers, the die cutting jigs. I abruptly suggest we call it a day.

Big Bob stretches. His face fills with mirth. "Tis a silly place." Bob is also a Monty Python fan. "Let's not go into the Big House."

"Well, this is it then," says the Gnome. We look at each other and realize that, indeed, our quest is at an end. "No need to worry about me. I can find my way home from here."

And as suddenly as he arrived at my home all those months ago, the Games Gnome is gone.

I feel satisfied, and empty, at the same time. As my "friend" Carl Jung once observed: "The meeting of two personalities is like the contact of two chemical substances: if there is any reaction, both are transformed."

EPILOGUE

It's been six months since I said goodbye to the Gnome that afternoon.

He seemed quite happy with our big adventure. Then I imagine, he flew off to his home "somewhere" in Europe. Of course, as he hurried off, he reminded me that he might "pop in" again without notice. But, so far, he hasn't.

But yesterday I got an envelope from a post box in Germany. I knew it must be from him!

The letter inside was, indeed, written in his flowing penmanship. A sealed packet accompanied it.

The letter began, "Dear Phil, regards to your better half." And being the ever-playful wit, the Gnome next says, "When you turn our excellent journey into a musical, here's my idea for the first verse of its theme song. It has got a rocking beat. One I am sure Big Bob would groove to."

> *In life there are rules: the dice have their say,*
> *The game is the thing, like Shakespeare's play.*
> *You best make a move and follow it through,*
> *If you don't play the game, the game will play you.*

I should have guessed the Gnome was also musically inclined.

The next pages of his letter evoke memories. "I have checked in, from time to time, with some of the friends who lent us a hand. Eric Sommersby has now played Cluedo games ending with three solutions not previously recorded in his notebook. He is delighted to say he won all three. Marion Nicé is working on a new theory of group thinking. She's calling it, 'The Crowd Learns to Think.'

"I hear the Sweeneys set a personal record at a Scrabble tournament in Darien, Connecticut. Gerald laid down QUIXORTY and scored a ton. Richard Levy is off to more remote countries. When I get really hungry, I am going back to Brussels to get in on a Risk game with General Perpose (or it is 'Porpoise'?). Meg got a promotion; well-deserved. And on the day after New Year's, Wally Zupan made a million in thirty minutes of trading!

"I still miss Victor Watson, rather terribly.

"Tim Grell is learning how to cook—which reminds me, you should take Rene Soriano out to lunch. You might get an idea for another book.

"Gonrad exercises influence over a regarded game company. Mike P. and Barbara just celebrated sixty great years. Sybille keeps very busy with her research, game playing and translation service. Oh, and you might tell your readers that she's been my wife since the end of 2007; we met when she delivered her talk on Catan at the Board Game Studies conference in Marburg, Germany. Our anniversary is the same day as Mike and Barbara's!

"I will leave you with some words from Voltaire. You know him. France. The Enlightenment. Eighteenth-century guy. Good with words.

Voltaire: real name François-Marie Arouet

"And I quote:'Each player must accept the cards life deals him or her; but once they are in hand, he or she alone must decide how to play [them] in order to win the game.'"

I've come to the letter's final page.The Gnome continues, "There is one more thing. I suspect that some of your readers will think you made me up out of thin air.They are likely to say, 'Phil, come on. There is no Games Gnome. He is just a figment.' So go ahead and open the packet. There is a photo inside. I would appreciate it if you could include it at the end just to prove to the doubters that I exist and have a real name.

The Games Gnome
Bruce Whitehill

The Honorary Gnome
Victor Watson

"Tra-la-la!"

Bruce

CREDITS AND ACKNOWLEDGMENTS

All photos, unless otherwise credited, are from the archives of Philip E. Orbanes and Bruce Whitehill.

I would like to thank the following individuals for their kind help in the preparation of this book:

Daniel and Ronnie Ducoff, Richard and Bettie Levy, Evelyn Anderson and Jenny Brown, Robert Reiss, Andrew P. Davis, Robert Hallowell, Rene Soriano, Randolph P. Barton, Everett "Mike" Morss, George Burtch, James Smart and from the Strong Museum of Play: Nic Ricketts Victoria Gray and Chris Bensch.

My wife Anna for her patience, proofreading, and encouragement.

To all who wished to remain anonymous—you know who you are; please know of my special appreciation.

To those who have passed on, including Joseph Milestone, Waldemar von Zedtwitz, Bernard Loomis, Louis Cheskin, Lynn Pressman, Silvia Noel and the late, great Victor Watson.

The Games Gnome would like to thank:

Hanne Kosinowski of Germany, Benjamin Aminzadah of Germany, Spartaco Albertarelli of Italy, Andy Grassie of Scotland, Mike Palatnik of the USA, Philip C. Orbanes of the USA, Nicolas Ricketts, and Shannon Symonds of the Strong Museum of Play, Rochester, NY

BIBLIOGRAPHY

*T*ortured *Cardboard* is based on the personal archives, collections, and experiences of the Games Gnome (Bruce Whitehill) and myself during our careers in the games business.

In the course of our research, we consulted certain printed and electronic resources for verification and clarification. The following is a list of the significant books, articles, and websites consulted.

Books:

Donovan, Tristan. *It's All a Game*, St, Martin's Press, New York, 2017

Convenevole, Roberto. *La Storia di Risiko*, Novecento Giochi, Rome, 2002

Orbanes, Philip. *The Game Makers*, Harvard Business School Press, 2003

Holland, Tim. *Better Backgammon*, David McKay Company, New York, 1974

Bradshaw, Jon. *Fast Company: How Six Master Gamblers Defy the Odds–and Always Win,* High Stakes, New York, 2003

Shea, James J. *It's All in the Game,* G.P. Putnam's Sons, New York, 1960

Fatsis, Stefan. *Word Freaks,* Penguin Books, New York, 2001

Mérő, László. *Moral Calculations,* Springer-Verlag, New York, 1998

Gunther, Max. *The Luck Factor,* Macmillan Publishing Co. Inc., New York 1977

Watson, Victor. *The Waddingtons Story,* Jeremy Mills Publishing, Huddersfield, West Yokrshire, England, 2008

Lowder, James (Ed.). *Family Games: The 100 Best,* Green Ronin Publishing, 2010; articles on CLUE (John Scott Tynes), THE GAME OF LIFE (Bruce C. Shelley), MONOPOLY (Steve Jackson), MOUSETRAP (Sheri Graner Ray), RISK (Peter Olotka), SCRABBLE (Richard Garfield).

Whitehill, Bruce. *Americanopoly—America as Seen Through its Games.* Lausanne, Switzerland: Musée Suisse du Jeu, 2004.

_____. *Games: American Boxed Games and Their Makers 1822-1992.* Radnor, PA: Wallace-Homestead/Chilton, 1992.

Articles:

Darrach, Brad. "The Day Bobby Blew It." 1973, *Playboy* magazine.

Dicter, Ernest. "How Word-of-Mouth Advertising Works," 1966, *Harvard Business Review*

Orbanes, Philip. "Everything I Know About Business I Learned from Monopoly." 2002, *Harvard Business Review*

Dansky, Richard. "Richard Dansky on The Settlers of Catan." *Hobby Games: The 100 Best,* edited by James Lowder, Green Ronin Publishing, 2007.

Garfield, Richard. "Richard Garfield on Dungeons & Dragons." *Hobby Games: The 100 Best*, edited by James Lowder, Green Ronin Publishing, 2007.

Weisman, Jordan. "Jordan Weisman on Magic:The Gathering." *Hobby Games: The 100 Best*, edited by James Lowder, Green Ronin Publishing, 2007.

Whitehill, Bruce. *American Games: A Historical Perspective*. Article in *Board Games Studies 2: The International Journal for the Study of Board Games*. Leiden, Netherlands: Research School, CNWS, Leiden University, 1999.

_____. "America's Classic Games." 2007, *Knucklebones* magazine.

_____. "American Games: A Historical Perspective." *The International Journal For the Study of Board Games*, Leiden University, 1999.

_____. "American Games:A Historical Perspective." Florence, Italy: *Board Games in Academia III*, 1999. Based on the proceedings of a colloquium held in Italy, April, 1999.

_____. "Ancient Amusements: Asia's Antediluvian distractions." *Asian Geographic*, 2010.

_____. "Bruce Whitehill on Careers." *Family Games:The 100 Best*, edited by James Lowder, Green Ronin Publishing, 2010.

_____. "Clue/Cluedo:The Full Story." Powerpoint presentation to the International Board Game Studies colloquium, 2012.

_____. "The Game of Kings, the King of Games" (Chess), 2007, *Knucklebones* magazine.

_____. "Games Timeline of the 20th Century." Dresher, PA: Game Researchers' Notes, Oct.-Dec., 1999.

_____. "Games: Cultural Recreation in the '50s—A Decade of Change." Wynantskill, NY: *The Ephemera Journal,* The

Ephemera Society of America, December, 1993. (Based on the oral presentation "American Games of the 1950s: How We Learned and Played," at the annual national meeting of the American Antiquarian Society, October, 1993).

_____. "Games of America, From Morality Through Monopoly," 2007, Musée Suisse du Jeu (Chapter for museum's anniversary book).

_____. "From WWII Through TV Land." 1997, *Toy Shop* magazine.

_____. "Halma and Chinese Checkers: Origins and Variations." *Step by Step: Proceedings of the 4th Colloquium, Board Games in Adacdemia*. Fribourg, Switzerland: Editions Universitaires Fribourg Suisse, 2002.

_____. "Halma and Chinese Checkers: Origins and Variations." Fribourg, Switzerland: *Step by Step, Proceedings of the 4th Colloquium of Board Games in Academia*, Editions Universitaires Fribourg, 2002.

_____. "Mah Jongg." Winter 2010, *AGPC Quarterly*, Association of Game & Puzzle Collectors.

_____. "The Royal Game." (Parcheesi), *Knucklebones* magazine, 2007.

_____. "The Story of Scrabble." *Games Annual* magazine, 1997.

Whitehill, Sybille. "The significance of players for the reception and further development of a contemporary game: 'The Settlers of Catan'." Talk given at the International Board Game Studies colloquium, 2003, Marburg, Germany.

_____. "Some reasons behind the success of 'The Settlers of Catan': What makes this contemporary board game so attractive to players?" Talk given at the International Board Game Studies colloquium, 2004, Philadelphia, PA.

_____. "The results of the 'Catan' surveys in Germany and the U.S.," 2006, published online at http://www.siedeln. de/phpBB/downloads.php?view=detail&id=91.

_____. "Die Ergebnisse der "Catan"-Umfragen in Deutschland und den USA," 2006, published online at www.siedeln.de.

Ellwood, Mark. "The Power of Play." 2018, *Bloomberg Pursuits.*

Websites and articles:

http://www.thebiggamehunter.comarticles

http:// wikipedia.org

https://www.historicgames.com/gamestimeline.html

https://www.nytimes.com/2010/03/17/us/17holland.html

https://thegammonpress.com/prince-alexis-obolensky-
the-father-of-modern-backgammon/

https://www.chessbazaar.com/blog/15-life-lessons-game-chess/

https://www.pcworld.com/article/2140220/the-
mainframe-turns-50-or-why-the-ibm-system360-
launch-was-the-dawn-of-enterprise-it.html

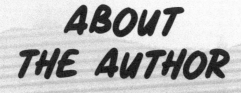

ABOUT
THE AUTHOR

PHOTO BY NATHAN MCGILVRAY

P hilip E. Orbanes began inventing games at age eight after playing Monopoly for the first time. He started his own game company as he entered college and sold it to a New York toy company before he graduated. Phil has been in the industry ever since, including three years running Ideal Toy's game division, eleven years as Senior VP of Research & Development at Parker Brothers, and twenty-five years as co-founder, president, and director of Winning Moves

Games—the leading maker of classic games sold through specialty retailing. Since 1979, he has served as chief judge at US and World Monopoly Championships. He has been interviewed dozens of times, and appeared on TV and in print (most recently in *Think* magazine).

PERMUTED PRESS
needs **you** to help

SPREAD (THE) INFECTION

FOLLOW US!

𝑓 | Facebook.com/PermutedPress
𝒚 | Twitter.com/PermutedPress

REVIEW US!

Wherever you buy our book, they can be reviewed! We want to know what you like!

GET INFECTED!

Sign up for our mailing list at
PermutedPress.com

PERMUTED
PRESS

KING ARTHUR AND THE KNIGHTS OF THE ROUND TABLE HAVE BEEN REBORN TO SAVE THE WORLD FROM THE CLUTCHES OF MORGANA WHILE SHE PROPELS OUR MODERN WORLD INTO THE MIDDLE AGES.

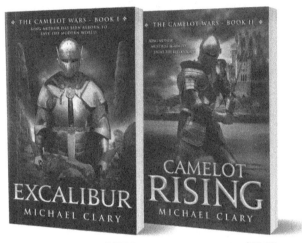

EAN 9781618685018 $15.99   **EAN** 9781682611562 $15.99

Morgana's first attack came in a red fog that wiped out all modern technology. The entire planet was pushed back into the middle ages. The world descended into chaos.

But hope is not yet lost— King Arthur, Merlin, and the Knights of the Round Table have been reborn.

PERMUTED
PRESS

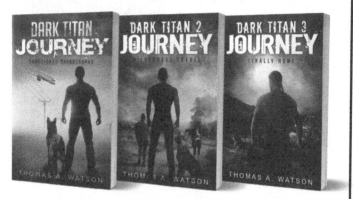

THE MORNINGSTAR STRAIN HAS BEEN LET LOOSE—IS THERE ANY WAY TO STOP IT?

EAN 9781618686497 $16.00

An industrial accident unleashes some of the Morningstar Strain. The doctor who discovered the strain and her assistant will have to fight their way through Sprinters and Shamblers to save themselves, the vaccine, and the base. Then they discover that it wasn't an accident at all—somebody inside the facility did it on purpose. The war with the RSA and the infected is far from over.

This is the fourth book in Z.A. Recht's The Morningstar Strain series, written by Brad Munson.

PERMUTED
PRESS

GATHERED TOGETHER AT LAST, THREE TALES OF FANTASY CENTERING AROUND THE MYSTERIOUS CITY OF SHADOWS...ALSO KNOWN AS CHICAGO.

EAN 9781682612286 $9.99   **EAN** 9781618684639 $5.99   **EAN** 9781618684899 $5.99

From *The New York Times* and *USA Today* bestselling author Richard A. Knaak comes three tales from Chicago, the City of Shadows. Enter the world of the Grey—the creatures that live at the edge of our imagination and seek to be real. Follow the quest of a wizard seeking escape from the centuries-long haunting of a gargoyle. Behold the coming of the end of the world as the Dutchman arrives.

Enter the City of Shadows.

PERMUTED
PRESS

WE CAN'T GUARANTEE THIS GUIDE WILL SAVE YOUR LIFE. BUT WE CAN GUARANTEE IT WILL KEEP YOU SMILING WHILE THE LIVING DEAD ARE CHOWING DOWN ON YOU.

EAN 9781618686695 $9.99

This is the only tool you need to survive the zombie apocalypse.

OK, that's not really true. But when the SHTF, you're going to want a survival guide that's not just geared toward day-to-day survival. You'll need one that addresses the essential skills for true nourishment of the human spirit. Living through the end of the world isn't worth a damn unless you can enjoy yourself in any way you want. (Except, of course, for anything having to do with abuse. We could never condone such things. At least the publisher's lawyers say we can't.)